Combined science

The practicals featured in this Lab Book follow the Combined Science Trilogy course numbering. If you are following the Synergy course, you can find the practical numbers in the table below.

AQA Practical name	Combined science: Trilogy required practical number	Combined science: Synergy required practical number
Microscopy	1	3
Osmosis	2	4
Food tests	3	7
Enzymes	4	20
Photosynthesis	5	10
Reaction time	6	8
Field investigations	7	12
Making salts	8	17
Electrolysis	9	21
Temperature changes	10	18
Rates of reaction	11	19
Chromatography	12	9
Water purification	13	11
Specific heat capacity	14	2
Resistance	15	16
Current–voltage characteristics	16	15
Density	17	1
Force and extension	18	13
Acceleration	19	14
Waves	20	5
Radiation and absorption	21	6

One of the first people to examine cells using a microscope was Robert Hooke. He examined bark from a cork oak tree and saw little box shapes. He called them 'cells' because he thought the boxes looked like the small rooms (or cells) that were found in monasteries at the time. Hooke realised that it was important to make accurate drawings of what he saw to help explain his work to others. You are going to examine specimens using a microscope and then make labelled drawings of them.

Your teacher may watch to see if you can:

- handle microscopes and slides carefully and safely.

AT links		Done
1	Use appropriate apparatus to record length and area.	
7	Use a microscope to make observations of biological specimens and produce labelled scientific drawings.	

Method 1: Examining pre-prepared slides of cells

A You will be changing the magnification of your microscope during this section of the practical. Use the box below to record all of your calculations. Set up your microscope on the lowest magnification objective lens. Work out the total magnification and measure the diameter of the field of view (by using the microscope to observe a transparent ruler). Record this in the box below.

B Put the next most powerful objective lens in place. Work out the magnification and by how much it has increased from the magnification in step **A** (e.g. moving from a ×10 to a ×50 is an increase of 5 times). Now divide the diameter of the field of view from step A by the increase in magnification to give you the new diameter of the field of view (e.g. if the field of view in step **A** was 2 mm, then 2 ÷ 5 = 0.4 mm). Do this for each objective lens. Record the total magnification and field of view diameter for each objective lens in the box below.

Aim

To use a microscope to observe cells and sub-cellular structures.

Apparatus

- light microscope
- lamp
- prepared slides
- transparent ruler

Safety ⚠

Handle slides with care.

AQA
GCSE Combined Science
Lab Book

Contents

Published by Pearson Education Limited, 80 Strand, London, WC2R 0RL.
www.pearsonschoolsandfecolleges.co.uk

Text © Mark Levesley, Penny Johnson, Sue Kearsey, Iain Brand, Carol Tear, Sue Robilliard and Pearson Education Limited 2017
Typeset and illustrated by Tech-Set Ltd Gateshead
Original illustrations © Pearson Education Limited 2015
Cover design by Pete Stratton
Cover photo/illustration © Shutterstock: Peter Reijners

First published 2017
19 18 17
10 9 8 7 6 5 4 3 2

British Library Cataloguing in Publication Data
A catalogue record for this book is available from the British Library

ISBN 978 1 292 208 275

Acknowledgements
The publishers would like to thank John Kavanagh for his contributions to the text.
The rights of Mark Levesley, Penny Johnson, Sue Kearsey, Iain Brand, Carol Tear, Sue Robilliard to be identified as authors of this work have been asserted by them in accordance with the Copyright, Designs and Patents Act 1988.

Note from the publisher
Pearson has robust editorial processes, including answer and fact checks, to ensure the accuracy of the content in this publication, and every effort is made to ensure this publication is free of errors. We are, however, only human, and occasionally errors do occur. Pearson is not liable for any misunderstandings that arise as a result of errors in this publication, but it is our priority to ensure that the content is accurate. If you spot an error, please do contact us at resourcescorrections@pearson.com so we can make sure it is corrected.

Having an investigative mind and carrying out experiments is fundamental to science. The AQA science curriculum has carefully selected practical work to:

- enhance the delivered content
- increase enthusiasm for the subject
- promote a more scientifically literate society
- enable students to gain vital transferable skills.

Completing these required practicals, along with other investigations selected by your teacher, enables you to have a rich hands-on experience of science as it is meant to be – a dynamic, practical subject relevant to everyone.

This Lab Book has been designed support your practical work, giving all the instructions you need to perform the required practicals, including apparatus and techniques (AT) skills self-assessment so that you can track your progress.

Every effort has been made to ensure coverage of the specification skills (WS – Working scientifically, AT – Use of apparatus and techniques), however, any method presented prevents fully completing WS 2.2 (Planning an investigation). WS 2.2 can also be covered if you plan an investigation prior to seeing the method presented. You can carry out your own plan, or adapt your plan using the method presented. Again, plans need to be risked assessed. It is hoped that the required practicals presented here are supplemented with other investigations and experiments that you complete through your GCSE course.

We have attempted to identify all the recognised hazards in the practical activities in this guide. The Activity and Assessment Pack provides suitable warnings about the hazards and suggests appropriate precautions. Teachers and technicians should remember, however, that where there is a hazard, the employer is required to carry out a risk assessment under either the COSHH Regulations or the Management of Health and Safety at Work Regulations. Most education employers have adopted a range of nationally available publications as model (general) risk assessments and, where such published assessments exist for the activity, our advice is believed to be compatible with them. We have assumed that practical work is carried out in a properly equipped and maintained laboratory and that any fieldwork takes account of the employer's guidelines. In particular, we have assumed that any mains-operated electrical equipment is properly maintained, that students have been shown how to conduct normal laboratory operations (such as heating or handling heavy objects) safely and that good practice is observed when chemicals or living organisms are handled (see below). We have also assumed that classes are sufficiently small and well-behaved for a teacher to be able to exercise adequate supervision of the students and that rooms are not so crowded that students' activities pose a danger to their neighbours.

CLEAPSS School Science Service are reviewing but not trialling this text. Following receipt of the CLEAPPS review any such guidance on how to make this resource conform to the above policy will be incorporated and the resources updated.

Important note

Neither Pearson, the authors nor the series editor take responsibility for the safety of any activity.

Before doing any practical activity you are legally required to carry out your own risk assessment. In particular, any local rules issued by your employer must be obeyed, regardless of what is recommended in this resource. Where students are required to write their own risk assessments they must always be checked by the teacher and revised, as necessary, to cover any issues the students may have overlooked. The teacher should always have the final control as to how the practical is conducted.

Further sources of information: CLEAPSS, www.cleapss.org.uk (includes Secondary Science Laboratory Handbook and Hazcards).

A note from the Publishers: This resource is based on the April 2016 accredited version of the specification. The worksheets in this resource have not been reviewed or endorsed by AQA and should not be considered as being published by AQA. Copies of official specifications for all AQA qualifications may be found on the website: www.aqa.org.uk

While the Publishers have made every attempt to ensure that advice on the qualification and its assessment is accurate, the official specification and associated assessment guidance materials are the only authoritative source of information and should always be referred to for definitive guidance.

C Now go back to the lowest magnification objective lens and observe a prepared slide.

D Use higher magnifications to observe the cells. Estimate the sizes using your field of view diameters.

E Using a sharp pencil, draw 4–5 cells in the box below. There is an example of how to do a microscope drawing in the box on the right. Identify and label the cells' parts. Use a ruler to draw your label lines. Write on the magnification. Add any sizes that you have estimated. Have a look for mitochondria (you may not find any as they are very difficult to see).

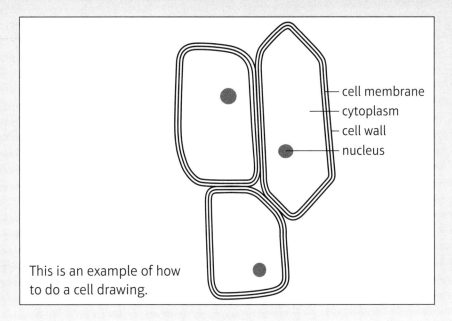

cell membrane
cytoplasm
cell wall
nucleus

This is an example of how to do a cell drawing.

Method 2: Examining your cheek cells

A   Using the pipette, add a small drop of water to the slide.

B   Stroke the inside of your cheek gently with the wooden spatula. You only want to collect loose cells, so do not scratch the inside of your mouth.

C   Use the end of the spatula that has been in your mouth to stir the drop of water on the slide. Place the used spatula in disinfectant.

D   Put on gloves and use a pipette to add a small drop of methylene blue stain. This makes cells easier to see.

E   Place a coverslip onto the slide at a 45° angle on one edge of the drop. Then use a toothpick to gently lower the coverslip down onto the drop, as shown in the diagram.

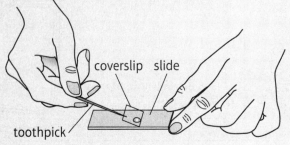

Avoid trapping air bubbles, which will appear as black-edged circles under a microscope.

F   Touch a piece of paper towel to any liquid that spreads out from under the coverslip.

G   Use the lowest magnification objective lens to observe the slide. The nuclei of the cheek cells will be dark blue.

H   Use higher magnifications to observe the cells. Estimate the sizes using your field of view diameters.

I   Using a sharp pencil, draw 4–5 cells in the box below. Identify and label the cells' parts. Use a ruler to draw your label lines. Write on the magnification. Add any sizes that you have estimated. Have a look for mitochondria (you may not find any as they are very difficult to see).

Apparatus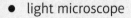

- light microscope
- lamp
- microscope slide
- coverslip
- methylene blue stain
- pipette
- paper towel
- water
- gloves
- wooden toothpick/ cocktail stick
- sterile wooden spatula/ tongue depressor
- disinfectant

Safety ⚠

Handle slides with care.

Anything that you have put into your mouth should be placed in disinfectant after use.

Wear gloves if using stains.

Wear eye protection.

Method 3: Examining onion cells

A Put on gloves and use a pipette to add a drop of iodine solution to a microscope slide.

B Using forceps, remove a very small piece of the thin 'skin' on the inside of the fleshy part of the onion. It is very thin indeed and quite tricky to handle.

C Place the small piece of skin on the drop of iodine on the slide.

D Place a coverslip onto the slide at a 45° angle on one edge of the drop. Then use a toothpick to gently lower the coverslip down onto the drop, as shown in the diagram. Avoid trapping air bubbles, which will appear as black-edged circles under a microscope.

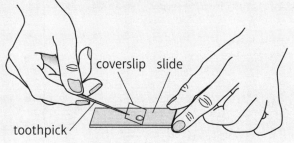
coverslip slide
toothpick

E Touch a piece of paper towel to any liquid that spreads out from under the coverslip.

F Use the lowest magnification objective lens to observe the slide. Then use higher magnifications to observe the cells in more detail. Estimate sizes as you observe.

G Using a sharp pencil, draw 4–5 cells in the box below. Identify and label the cells' parts. Use a ruler to draw your label lines. Write on the magnification. Add any sizes that you have estimated. Have a look for mitochondria (you may not find any as they are very difficult to see).

Apparatus

- light microscope
- lamp
- microscope slide
- coverslip
- iodine stain
- pipette
- paper towel
- forceps
- wooden toothpick/cocktail stick
- piece of onion bulb
- gloves

Safety ⚠

Handle slides and microscopes with care.

Wear gloves if using stains.

Wear eye protection.

Osmosis is the overall movement of water molecules from a region where there are more of them in a particular volume to a region where there are fewer, through a semi-permeable membrane. The cells in a potato contain many substances dissolved in water. The cells are surrounded by cell membranes that are permeable to water. When a strip of potato is placed in a solution, the overall movement of water molecules between the potato cells and the solution will depend on which has the higher concentration of solutes. In this practical, you will investigate osmosis in potato strips in terms of the percentage change in mass of potato in different solutions.

Your teacher may watch to see if you can:

- measure accurately
- work carefully.

AT links		Done
1	Use appropriate apparatus to record mass and time.	
3	Use appropriate apparatus and techniques to observe and measure the process of osmosis.	
5	Measure the rate of osmosis by water uptake.	

Method

A Using the waterproof pen, label each tube with the name of one of the solutions. Place the boiling tubes in the rack.

B Dry a potato strip carefully by blotting it with a paper towel. Measure its mass on the balance. The potato strips can be removed using a cork borer, as shown in the diagram, or cut using a scalpel. This will have been done for you, before the experiment.

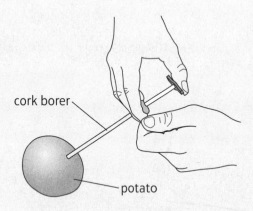

cork borer

potato

C Place the potato strip into one of the tubes. Record the label on the tube and the mass of the strip in your results table (see next page).

D Repeat steps **B** and **C** until all strips have been measured and placed in tubes.

E Carefully fill each tube with the appropriate solution, so that the potato is fully covered. Leave the tubes for at least 15 minutes.

F Use the forceps to remove each potato strip from its tube, blot dry on a paper towel and measure its mass again. Record all the masses in the results table.

Aim

To investigate how solution concentration affects percentage change in mass of potato strips due to osmosis.

Apparatus

- four potato strips
- accurate balance
- four boiling tubes and rack (or beakers)
- waterproof pen
- four sucrose solutions: 0%, 40%, 80%, 100%
- forceps
- paper towels

Safety ⚠

Do not drink any of the solutions or eat the potatoes.

Prediction

1 For each of the four solutions you will use, predict whether the potato strips will gain mass, lose mass or keep the same mass. Explain your predictions. Record your predictions and explanations in the box below.

Recording your results

2 Complete the first three columns of the table below, labelled Solution, **A** and **B** with the solution descriptions and your measurements from the experiment.

Solution	A Mass of potato strip at start (g)	B Mass of potato strip at end (g)	C Change in mass (g) = B – A	D % change in mass $= \frac{C}{A} \times 100\%$

3 Complete column **C** by calculating the change in mass for each potato strip using the formula shown.

4 Complete column **D** by calculating the percentage change in mass for each potato strip using the formula shown.

5 Compare the results for percentage change in mass from all groups in the class. For each solution, identify any results that seem very different from the others (outliers). Try to suggest a reason why they are so different.

6 Using all results except outliers, calculate a mean value for percentage change in mass for each solution.

7 Draw a suitable chart or graph to show the mean percentage change in the mass of each potato strip on the *y*-axis against the solution description on the *x*-axis.

Considering your results/conclusions

8 Describe and explain the pattern shown in your chart or graph.
Use the word 'osmosis' in your answer.

9 Explain why you calculated percentage change in mass.

10 Explain why calculating a mean value from several repeats of the same experiment is more likely to give a value that can be reproduced by others.

Evaluation

11 Describe any problems that you had with the experiment. Suggest how these could be reduced or avoided to produce better results.

By law, all packaged food and drink must be labelled to show how much fat, sugar, protein and some other substances it contains. This is to help customers make informed choices about what they eat and drink. Every new food or drink that is developed must be tested to produce the information needed for the labelling. You will be given a range of powdered foods. Use the food tests below to identify whether each food contains the substances that the reagents test for. Use your results to help you identify the foods from the list you are given. Remember to wipe the spatula and stirrer clean between tests (using a paper towel) to prevent cross-contamination.

Your teacher may watch to see if you can:

- follow instructions carefully
- work safely, reducing the risk of harm from hazards.

AT links		Done
2	Safe use of a Bunsen burner and a boiling water bath.	

Method

Iodine test for starch

A Place one spatula of powdered food on a dish.

B Using a dropper, place a few drops of iodine solution onto the food.

C Record the letter of the food and any change in the colour of the solution.

Benedict's test for reducing sugars

D Place two spatulas of powdered food into a test tube. Add about $1\,cm^3$ of water to the tube and stir to mix.

E Add an equal volume of Benedict's solution and mix.

F Place the tube in a water bath at about 95 °C for a few minutes.

G Record the letter of the food and the colour of the solution.

Biuret test for protein

H Place two spatulas of powdered food into a test tube. Add about $1\,cm^3$ of water to the tube and stir to mix.

I Add an equal volume of potassium hydroxide solution to the tube and stir.

J Add two drops of copper sulfate solution and stir.

K Record the letter of the food and the colour of the solution after a few minutes.

Emulsion test for lipids

L Place two spatulas of powdered food into a test tube.

M Add $2\,cm^3$ of ethanol to the tube. Place a bung firmly in the end of the tube and shake the tube vigorously.

N Allow the contents to settle.

O Pour the liquid from the top of the mixture into a test tube half-filled with water.

P Record the letter of the food and whether the water is cloudy or clear.

Aim

To identify starch, reducing sugars, proteins and lipids in foods.

Apparatus

- eye protection
- water
- measuring cylinder
- spatula
- powdered foods
- paper towels
- test tubes, racks and bungs
- stirrer
- iodine solution in dropper bottle
- Benedict's solution
- potassium hydroxide solution
- copper sulfate solution
- ethanol
- cold water
- water bath at 95 °C

Safety ⚠

Wear eye protection.
Wash any splashes from skin quickly.
Do not taste any of the food substances.
Potassium hydroxide can be harmful to skin and eyes.
Avoid scalding with hot water.

Recording your results

1   Record your results in the table. There is space below the table to add more rows if needed.

Food	Colour at end of ...			
	iodine test	Benedict's test	biuret test	emulsion test
A				
B				
C				
D				

Considering your results/conclusions

2   Which foods contained:

   a   starch

   b   reducing sugar

   c   protein

   d   lipid?

Evaluation

3   Identify any problems you had with this experiment. Explain how the method could be improved to reduce or avoid these errors.

Amylase is an enzyme made in the salivary glands in your mouth and in the pancreas. It catalyses the breakdown of starch into smaller sugar molecules. The iodine test identifies the presence of starch, but does not react with sugar. You will use this test to show how effective amylase is in digesting starch at different pHs.

Your teacher may watch to see if you can:
- work safely
- collect accurate data.

AT links		Done
1	Use appropriate apparatus to record the volumes of liquids, time and pH.	
2	Safe use of a water bath or electric heater.	
5	Measure the rate of reaction by the colour change of iodine indicator.	

Method

A Drop one drop of iodine solution into each depression of the dimple tile.

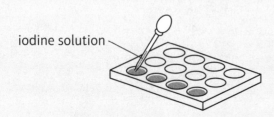

iodine solution

B Use a syringe to measure 2 cm³ of amylase solution into a test tube.

C Add 1 cm³ of your pH solution to the test tube using a second syringe. Record the pH of the solution that you are using.

D Using a third syringe, add 2 cm³ of starch solution to the mixture and start the stop clock. Use the pipette to stir the mixture.

E After 20 seconds, take a small amount of the mixture in the pipette and place one drop of it on the first iodine drop on the tile. Return the rest of the solution in the pipette to the test tube.

F If the iodine solution turns black, there is still starch in the mixture and you should repeat step **E** after 10 seconds. If the iodine solution remains yellow, all the starch has been digested and you should record the time taken for this to happen.

G If there is time, repeat the experiment using a solution with a different pH.

Aim

To investigate the effect of pH on the rate of digestion of starch by amylase.

Apparatus

- iodine solution in dropping bottle
- dimple tile
- test tubes
- test tube rack
- syringes
- pipette
- amylase solution
- starch solution
- solutions of specific pH
- stop clock

Safety ⚠
Eye protection should be worn.

Prediction

1   Predict at which pH the amylase will digest starch fastest. Explain your prediction.
    Record your prediction and explanation in the box below.

Recording your results

2   Draw a table in the box below, to present these results clearly.

3   Collect data from all the groups in the class so that you have results for each of the different
    pHs. If you have more than one result for any pH, calculate the mean time. Record the mean
    times in the box below.

Considering your results

4 In the space below, plot a line graph to show the time taken for amylase to digest starch at different pHs.

5 Look at your graph and use it to describe the effect of pH on the time taken for amylase to digest starch.

6 Suggest a reason for the shape of your graph.

Evaluation

7 Describe any problems you had when carrying out the experiment.

8 Suggest reasons for these problems and suggest how the method could be changed to help reduce them.

9 Were any of the results surprising? If so, why?

10 Do you think you have enough results to support your conclusion? Explain your answer.

Microscopic algae have cells that contain chloroplasts, like plant leaf cells. The algae can be trapped in jelly balls to make them easier to handle. You will put algal balls in an indicator that changes colour as carbon dioxide levels change. Under normal conditions the indicator is a red colour, but this changes to yellow at higher carbon dioxide concentrations and purple at lower carbon dioxide concentrations.[1]

Your teacher may watch to see if you can:

- follow instructions carefully
- work safely.

AT links		Done
1	Use appropriate apparatus to record the rate of change of carbon dioxide levels; and to measure and control the temperature of the water in the 'heat shield' beaker.	
2	Safe use of a thermometer to measure and control temperature of water bath.	
3	Use appropriate apparatus and techniques to observe and measure the process of change of carbon dioxide levels.	
4	Safe and ethical use and disposal of living aquatic organism to measure physiological functions and responses to light.	
5	Measuring rate of reaction by colour change of indicator according to pH.	

Aim

To find out how light intensity affects the **rate** of photosynthesis.

Apparatus

- eye protection
- bijou bottles and caps
- beaker of algal balls
- hydrogencarbonate indicator
- lamp and heat filter
- metre rule
- measuring cylinder
- kitchen foil
- stop clock
- plastic forceps/spoon

Safety ⚠

Wear eye protection.

Wash your hands after setting up the experiment.

Avoid touching the hot lamp.

Method

A Decide the different distances you are going to use between the algae and the lamp. You will need one clear glass bottle for each distance. You will also need one extra bottle.

B Add 10–15 algal balls to each bottle.

C Add the same volume of indicator solution to each bottle and put on the bottle caps.

D Your teacher will have a chart or a range of bottles showing the colours of the indicator at different pHs. Compare the colour in your bottles with this pH range to work out the pH at the start.

E Set up a heat filter between the lamp and where you will place your bottles. The heat filter is a water-filled bottle or other clear container. Take great care not to spill water near the lamp.

F Cover one bottle in kitchen foil, so that it is in the dark.

G Place your bottles at measured distances from the lamp. Put the bottle covered in kitchen foil next to the bottle that is closest to the lamp.

H Turn on the lamp and time 60 minutes (or longer).

I Compare the colours of all your bottles with those of the pH range bottles.

J Record the pHs of the solutions in your bottles in a suitable table.

K For each bottle, calculate the change in pH per hour. Add these calculations to your table.

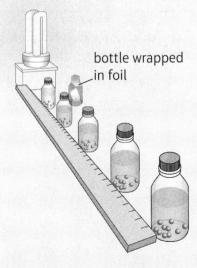

bottle wrapped in foil

[1]A note to teachers: The full title of this required practical is to "Investigate the effect of light intensity on the rate of photosynthesis using an aquatic organism such as pondweed." The traditional method uses counting bubbles of oxygen or measuring the gas produced using pondweed and schools may also wish to carry out this experiment to fulfil AQA's criteria. However, the practical given here has proved to be a more successful variant of investigating light intensity.

Recording your results

1 Record your results in the table below.

Distance from lamp to bottle (cm)	pH at start	pH at end	Rate of photosynthesis (change in pH/hour)

Considering your results/conclusions

2 a For each bottle, calculate the rate of photosynthesis as the change in pH per hour.

change in pH = pH at end – pH at start

$$\text{rate} = \frac{\text{change in pH}}{\text{time (in hours)}}$$

b Use your calculations to complete the last column of the table above.

3 Plot your results on a scatter graph. Plot the variable that you have changed (the independent variable) on the x-axis. Plot the rate of photosynthesis on the y-axis.

Considering your results/conclusions

4 **a** Describe the pattern shown on your graph.

b Explain why this pattern is observed.

5 **H** Explain whether the pattern on your graph obeys the **inverse square law**.

Evaluation

6 Explain the purpose of the tube covered in foil.

Combined science

We need to respond to changes in our environment. Sometimes these responses need to be rapid so that we are protected from an imminent threat, for example an object travelling towards us very quickly. The time taken for us to react is known as our reaction time. You are going to undertake a simple investigation into reaction times. You are going to analyse the results to see if faster reaction times can be linked to skills or experiences, e.g. being proficient at reactive computer games.

Your teacher may watch to see if you can:

- follow instructions carefully
- work safely.

AT links		Done
1	Use appropriate apparatus to record time.	
3	Selecting appropriate apparatus and techniques to measure the process of reaction time.	
4	Safe and ethical use of humans to measure physiological function of reaction time and responses to a chosen factor.	

Aim

To find out who has the fastest reactions.

Apparatus

- metre rule
- bench or table
- chair or stool
- a partner

Safety ⚠

When the ruler is falling, it could fall in different directions. Take care that it does not hit anyone.

Method

A The person who is having their reactions tested should sit down on the chair with their weaker arm (the opposite to the one that they normally write with) placed on the table. Their hand should be overhanging the table edge.

B The tester holds a ruler vertically between the outstretched index finger thumb of the person being tested. The finger and thumb should not be touching the ruler. The top of the thumb should be level with the zero mark on the ruler.

C The tester releases the ruler without telling the person being tested. The person being tested has to catch the ruler as quickly as possible.

D When the person catches the ruler, record the number that is level with the top of their hand. Record the length of the drop in the table below. Repeat the drop five times and calculate an average.

E Now swap roles.

F Find out who has the fastest reaction time. There are two extra columns in case your group is larger than two.

Drop	Person 1	Person 2	Person 3	Person 4
First drop				
Second drop				
Third drop				
Fourth drop				
Fifth drop				
Average drop				

Considering your results/conclusions

1   Draw a suitable graph or chart to show your results.

2 a Who had the fastest reaction time?

b Is there any reason why this person should have the fastest reaction time?
(Hint: Does this person play lots of video games, or are they good at reaction sports?)

3 Did the reaction times get quicker from the first drop to the fifth drop?
. Explain any pattern you can see in your results.

Evaluation

4 What could you do to improve this experiment?

5 Think of a different way to test reaction times.

A transect is used to study the distribution of organisms and how it is affected by changes in environmental conditions. With a belt transect, quadrats are placed at regular intervals along the transect line to sample the organisms. You will use a belt transect to study the effect of abiotic factors on the abundance of low-growing plants. The transect will stretch between open ground and heavy shade under a large tree. Several abiotic factors will vary along the transect. Before you start, you will need to decide which abiotic factors to measure and how to measure them. You will also need to decide which plants to record and how you will record their abundance within each quadrat.

Your teacher may watch to see if you can:

- work efficiently
- follow safety guidance.

AT links		Done
1	Use appropriate apparatus to record length and area.	
3	Use transect lines and quadrats to measure distribution of a species.	
4	Safe and ethical use of organisms and response to a factor in the environment.	
6	Application of appropriate sampling techniques to investigate the distribution and abundance of organisms in an ecosystem via direct use in the field.	

Method

A You are going to investigate the distribution of a particular plant species. Choose from: dandelions, daisies or buttercups. (Your teacher might suggest an alternative plant that is found in the local area.) If your teacher has not told you where to place the transect, look for somewhere that shows obvious variation in environmental conditions, such as from bright light to deep shade under a tree, or from an area that shows heavy trampling to an area with less trampling.

B Decide which environmental factors you will measure and how you will measure them.

C Peg out the tape measure along the ground to form the transect line.

D Take measurements at regular intervals along the transect line (as shown in the diagram). Decide on your measurement intervals, which may depend on how long the line is and how much time you have to record information.

E Place the top left-hand corner of the quadrat at a measurement point on the transect line.

F Measure the environmental factors at that point and record them.

G Record the abundance of your selected organism (this is the plant species you chose earlier) in the quadrat.

H Repeat steps **F** and **G** at each measurement point along the transect.

Aim

To investigate the distribution of a species using a transect and quadrats.

Apparatus

- long tape measure (at least 20 m) with pegs at each end
- quadrat (e.g. 50 cm × 50 cm square)
- apparatus for measuring suitable abiotic factors, e.g. light sensor and recorder, soil humidity sensor, anemometer (wind speed measurer)
- optional: identification charts and pencil

Safety ⚠

Follow any safety guidance related to the working area.

Consider the safety aspects of your chosen site, such as poisonous plants, animal faeces or open water, and take appropriate precautions while working.

Wash your hands after the experiment.

Recording your results

1 In the space below, draw a table to record the abundance of the organism you sampled at each point along the transect line, as well as the environmental factor measurements at each point.

No Daisies	Brightness / lux or Distance / m
15	599
5	650
5	6 2 3
8	607
8	705
	7 3 1

2 Draw a suitable chart or graph to show your results.

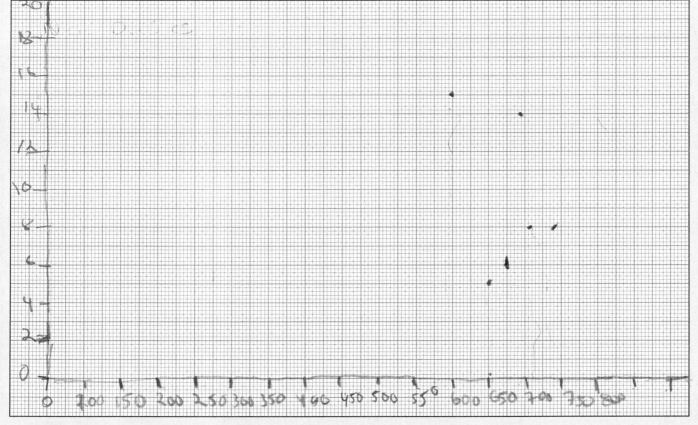

Considering your results/conclusions

3 Describe the change in distribution of your chosen organism along the transect.

4 Describe the change in your chosen environmental factor along the transect.

5 Describe any correlation between the change in distribution of the organism and the change in environmental factor.

6 Suggest an explanation for any correlation that you have described in **5**.

Evaluation

7 Describe an experiment you could do in the lab to test whether the environmental factor you measured affects the organism as you suggest in your answer to question **6**.

Salts, such as copper sulfate, are compounds formed by reacting an acid with a base. Copper oxide reacts with warm sulfuric acid to produce a blue solution of the salt copper sulfate. In this practical, you will use these reactants to prepare pure, dry, hydrated copper sulfate crystals.

Your teacher may watch to see if you can:

- safely and correctly use apparatus.

AT links		Done
2	Safe use of appropriate heating devices and techniques including use of a Bunsen burner and a water bath or electric heater.	
3	Use of appropriate apparatus and techniques for conducting chemical reactions, including appropriate reagents.	
4	Safe use of a range of equipment to purify and/or separate chemical mixtures including evaporation, filtration, crystallisation.	
6	Safe use and careful handling of liquids and solids, including careful mixing of reagents under controlled conditions.	

Method

A Wearing goggles, pour about 40 cm³ of dilute sulfuric acid into a beaker.

B Set up the gauze, tripod and heatproof mat. Using the Bunsen burner, heat the acid *gently* until it is almost boiling. Turn off the Bunsen burner.

C Use the spatula to add a little copper oxide to the acid and stir.

D Keep repeating step **C** until the black powder does not disappear after stirring. (This makes sure the copper oxide is in excess.)

E Filter the mixture into a beaker and pour into an evaporating basin.

F Place the evaporating basin on top of a beaker half full of water. Heat the beaker, evaporating basin and contents using a Bunsen burner on a blue flame.

G Heat until about half of the water has evaporated. Then allow the evaporating basin to cool.

H When cool, transfer the solution to a Petri dish or watch glass and leave for a few days to allow the water to evaporate.

I Observe the shape and colour of the copper sulfate crystals formed.

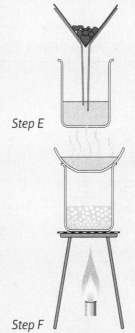

Step E

Step F

Aim

To prepare a sample of pure, dry, hydrated copper sulfate crystals from copper oxide.

Apparatus

- safety goggles
- 250 cm³ beaker
- 100 cm³ beaker
- Bunsen burner
- gauze and tripod
- heatproof mat
- Petri dish or watch glass
- 100 cm³ measuring cylinder
- evaporating basin
- spatula
- stirring rod
- filter funnel
- filter paper
- tongs
- dilute sulfuric acid
- copper(II) oxide

Safety ⚠

Wear safety goggles at all times.

Recording your results

1 Describe the colour, shape and size of the copper sulfate crystals produced.

2 Describe the appearance of:

a the sulfuric acid

b the copper oxide

c the solution at the end of the reaction.

Considering your results

3 Write a word equation to show the reaction you have carried out.

4 State why you need to be sure excess copper oxide is added in step **D**.

5 Name the substance left in the filter paper in step **E**.

6 What is dissolved in the solution that went through the filter paper?

7 Explain why this is an example of a neutralisation reaction.

8 What substance acts as a base in this reaction?

9 Write a symbol equation to show the reaction you have carried out. Include the state symbols.
Use your answer to question **3** to help you.

The electrolysis of molten or dissolved ionic salts is carried out using inert (unreactive) electrodes (usually graphite or platinum). When a molten salt is electrolysed, ions are discharged as atoms or molecules at the electrodes. However, electrolysis of dissolved ionic salts is more complex. This is because water ionises to a very small extent, so in an aqueous solution of a salt there are some hydrogen ions (H^+) and hydroxide ions (OH^-), as well as the ions of the dissolved solid. You are going to predict the substances formed at electrodes when different substances are electrolysed. You will then carry out the electrolysis of these substances to confirm whether you were right.

Your teacher may watch to see if you can:
- follow instructions carefully
- work safely.

AT links		Done
3	Use of appropriate apparatus and techniques for conducting and monitoring chemical reactions.	
7	Use of appropriate apparatus and techniques to draw, set up and use electrochemical cells for separation and production of elements and compounds.	

Aim
To investigate the substances that are formed at the electrodes when different salt solutions are electrolysed.

Apparatus
- safety goggles
- copper(II) sulfate solution
- sodium chloride solution
- carbon electrodes
- 100 cm³ beaker
- Petri dish lid
- tweezers
- connecting leads
- copper(II) chloride solution
- sodium sulfate solution
- low voltage power supply
- damp litmus paper
- electrode holder

Safety
Safety goggles need to be worn throughout the practical.

Hypothesis
Write down your hypothesis. Explain why you made this hypothesis.

Prediction

Now that you have studied work on electrolysis, predict what products will be formed at each electrode and give your reasons.

Solution	Positive electrode	Negative electrode	Why I think this...
copper(II) chloride			(positive electrode)
			(negative electrode)
copper(II) sulfate			(positive electrode)
			(negative electrode)
sodium chloride			(positive electrode)
			(negative electrode)
sodium sulfate			(positive electrode)
			(negative electrode)

Method

A Place about 50 cm³ of copper(II) chloride solution into a 100 cm³ beaker.

B Insert the carbon electrodes into the electrode holder and place this into the copper(II) chloride solution.

C Use the leads to connect the electrodes to the low voltage power supply. Make sure you connect the electrodes to the d.c. terminals. These are normally coloured red and black.

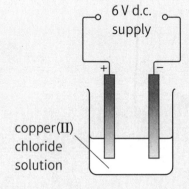

D Set the voltage to 6 V and switch on.

E Look at the electrodes. Is anything happening? There could be a colour change or fizzing.

F Hold a piece of damp litmus paper close to the electrode that is bubbling. (This should be the positive electrode.) What do you see happening? Add this information to your results table on the next page.

G After a few minutes, switch off the low voltage supply and take a closer look at the other electrode. (This should be the negative electrode.) Is there a colour change? Record any information in your results table.

H Remove the liquid from the beaker. Your teacher will tell you where to put this. You will need to clean both electrodes. Rinsing them under running water should be fine.

I Repeat steps **A** to **H** using the other solutions.

Combined science

Considering your results/conclusions

1 Make sure your table below is complete. Don't forget to write in your evidence.

Solution	Positive electrode	Negative electrode	Evidence for this...
copper(II) chloride			(positive electrode)
			(negative electrode)
copper(II) sulfate			(positive electrode)
			(negative electrode)
sodium chloride			(positive electrode)
			(negative electrode)
sodium sulfate			(positive electrode)
			(negative electrode)

2 Compare your final results to the predictions you made at the start. How accurate were your predictions?

....
....

3 The test for chlorine is that it bleaches damp litmus paper. The other two gases you are likely to have found would need additional tests to confirm what they are. Write down the names and the tests for these gases.

....
....
....
....
....

During a chemical reaction, energy is transferred between the reacting substances and their surroundings. This energy transfer is usually by heating, particularly if a reaction takes place in solution. The stored thermal (heat) energy in the solution increases during an exothermic reaction, and decreases during an endothermic reaction. This means you can determine whether a reaction in solution is exothermic or endothermic:

- the temperature increases in an exothermic reaction
- the temperature decreases in an endothermic reaction.

You are going to investigate a type of reaction known as a neutralisation reaction.

Your teacher may watch to see if you can:
- follow instructions carefully
- work safely.

AT links		Done
1	Use of appropriate apparatus to make and record a range of measurements accurately, including mass, temperature, and volume of liquids.	
3	Use of appropriate apparatus and techniques for conducting and monitoring chemical reactions.	
5	Making and recording of appropriate observations during chemical reactions including changes in temperature.	
6	Safe use and careful handling of gases, liquids and solids, including careful mixing of reagents under controlled conditions, using appropriate apparatus to explore chemical changes.	

Aim
To react hydrochloric acid with sodium hydroxide solution in a neutralisation reaction and measure the temperature change.

Apparatus
- two polystyrene cups
- 250 cm³ beaker
- lid for one cup
- measuring cylinders
- sodium hydroxide
- hydrochloric acid
- tripod
- thermometer
- safety goggles

Safety ⚠
Wear safety goggles.
Sodium hydroxide and hydrochloric acid at this concentration are corrosive and very damaging to eyes.

Hypothesis
Write down your hypothesis for this experiment. This hypothesis could include a sketch graph.

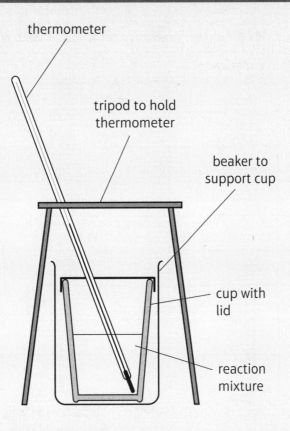

Method

A Use a measuring cylinder to put 30 cm³ of 2.0 mol/dm³ hydrochloric acid into a polystyrene cup.

B Clean out the measuring cylinder with water.

C Place the polystyrene cup into a glass beaker to make it more stable. Take the temperature of the acid and write this in your results table. This should go in the column for experiment 1.

D Use the measuring cylinder to put 40 cm³ of 2.0 mol/dm³ sodium hydroxide solution into a second polystyrene cup.

E Remove 5 cm³ of 2.0 mol/dm³ sodium hydroxide solution from your 40 cm³ measured out in step **D**.

F Add this to the polystyrene cup containing the acid. Put the lid on the cup containing the mixture and stir with the thermometer. Enclose the thermometer with a tripod to stop the cup and thermometer falling over.

G Keep stirring until the temperature reaches a maximum and starts to fall. Record the highest temperature in your table.

H Repeat steps **E**–**G** until all the 40 cm³ has been added.

I When you have finished, rinse out your cups and measuring cylinders and repeat the experiment at least one more time. If time is short, you could use results from other groups because everyone will have used the same amounts and the same strengths of solutions.

Considering your results/conclusions

1 Record your results in the table on the following page. There are some extra columns for repeated results from your experiments or results from other groups. To calculate the mean, add up all the results in a row and divide by the number of results in the row.

Volume of sodium hydroxide solution added (cm³)	Maximum temperature recorded at each stage (°C)				
	Experiment 1	Experiment 2			Mean
0					
5					
10					
15					
20					
25					
30					
35					
40					

2   On the next page, draw a graph of your results with the volume of sodium hydroxide solution added (cm³) (the independent variable) on the x-axis and the mean maximum temperature (°C) (the dependent variable) on the y-axis.

3   Draw two straight lines of best fit. One will be through all the points which are increasing in temperature and the other will be through all the points which are decreasing in temperature. You need to make sure the lines cross, so you might need to extend them. The diagram to the right should give you an idea what this should look like.

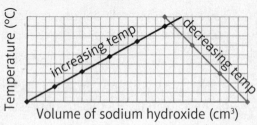

4   What volumes of hydrochloric acid and sodium hydroxide would produce the largest temperature rise?

5   Why does the temperature start to fall towards the end of the experiment?

Evaluation

6   How could you make the data you collect from this investigation more accurate?

7   It is difficult to find the exact volume of sodium hydroxide solution that would give the maximum temperature rise. What further work would need to be carried out to find this exact volume of sodium hydroxide?

AQA GCSE
Combined science
Practical 11: Rates of reaction
(Part 1: Measuring gas production)

The progress of a chemical reaction can be measured by how the amounts of reactant or product change with time, or by the time taken for the reaction to reach a certain point.

You are going to investigate the reaction between hydrochloric acid and marble chips (calcium carbonate), to find out how the concentration of the acid affects the rate. You will monitor the progress of the reaction by measuring the volume of carbon dioxide produced.

Part 1: Measuring gas production
Your teacher may watch to see if you can:
- carefully control variables during investigations
- measure change accurately.

	AT links	Done
1	Use of appropriate apparatus to make and record a range of measurements accurately, including mass, temperature, and volume of liquids.	
3	Use of appropriate apparatus and techniques for conducting and monitoring chemical reactions.	
5	Making and recording of appropriate observations during chemical reactions including changes in temperature.	
6	Safe use and careful handling of gases, liquids and solids, including careful mixing of reagents under controlled conditions, using appropriate apparatus to explore chemical changes.	

Aim
To investigate the effect on the rate of reaction of changing the concentration of solutions by measuring the production of a gas.

Apparatus
- eye protection
- balance
- water trough
- 100 cm^3 measuring cylinder
- stop clock
- conical flask
- delivery tube and bung
- marble chips
- 1.0 mol/dm^3 and 2.0 mol/dm^3 hydrochloric acid

Safety ⚠
Wear eye protection at all times.

Care is needed with acid solutions. Wash off splashes immediately.

Hypothesis
Write down your hypothesis. Explain your hypothesis.

Method
A Set up the apparatus as shown in the diagram.

B Measure 40 cm^3 of 2.0 mol/dm^3 hydrochloric acid into a conical flask.

C Add 5 g of marble chips to the flask.

D Immediately stopper the flask and start the stop clock.

E Note the total volume of gas produced after every 30 seconds for five minutes or until the reaction has finished.

F Repeat steps A–E using 1.0 mol/dm^3 hydrochloric acid.

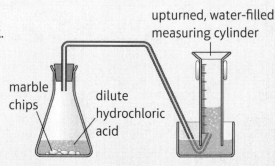

upturned, water-filled measuring cylinder

marble chips

dilute hydrochloric acid

Recording your results

1 Record your results in the table below.

Time (min)	0	0.5	1.0	1.5	2.0	2.5	3.0	3.5	4.0	4.5	5.0
2.0 mol/dm³ hydrochloric acid											
1.0 mol/dm³ hydrochloric acid											

Considering your results/conclusion

2 Draw a scatter diagram for both sets of results on the same graph. The volume of gas produced in cm³ (the dependent variable) should be on the y-axis. The time in minutes (the independent variable) should be on the x-axis. Use different coloured lines for each concentration of acid.

3 Explain how you can tell from the scatter diagrams when the reactions were finished.

4 Describe how increasing the concentration affects the rate of reaction.

5 Explain how your results and scatter diagrams fit with your conclusion in question **4**.

Evaluation

6 Suggest possible sources of error in this investigation.

7 Suggest possible changes to the method that could improve the reliability of the results.

AQA GCSE
Combined science
Practical 11: Rates of reaction
(Part 2: Observing a colour change)

Part 2: Observing a colour change

The progress of a chemical reaction can be measured by how amounts of reactant or product change with time, or by the time taken for the reaction to reach a certain point.

You are going to investigate the effect of concentration on the rate of reaction between sodium thiosulfate and hydrochloric acid. You will monitor the progress of the reaction by observing a colour change.

Your teacher may watch to see if you can:

- carefully control variables during investigations
- measure change accurately
- work safely.

Hypothesis

Write down your hypothesis. Explain your hypothesis.

Aim

To investigate the effect of changing the concentration on the rate of reaction between sodium thiosulfate and hydrochloric acid, by observing a colour change in the solutions.

Apparatus

- eye protection
- 250 cm³ conical flask
- 10 cm³ measuring cylinder
- 50 cm³ measuring cylinder
- stop clock
- test tube
- test tube rack
- white paper with cross
- sodium thiosulfate solution
- dilute hydrochloric acid

Safety ⚠

Wear eye protection at all times.

Care is needed with acid solutions. Wash off splashes immediately.

Take care to avoid breathing in any sulfur dioxide fumes.

Method

A Place 10 cm³ of sodium thiosulfate solution and 40 cm³ of water into a 250 cm³ conical flask.

B Measure 10 cm³ of dilute hydrochloric acid into a measuring cylinder.

C Place the conical flask (containing the previously measured out sodium thiosulfate and water) on a piece of white paper marked with a cross, as shown opposite.

D Add the acid to the thiosulfate and start the stop clock.

E Looking down from above, stop the clock when the cross disappears.

F Note this time.

G Repeat steps **A–F**, replacing with the replacing the original amounts of sodium thiosulfate and water in step A with the following:
20 cm³ sodium thiosulfate + 30 cm³ water
30 cm³ sodium thiosulfate + 20 cm³ water
40 cm³ sodium thiosulfate + 10 cm³ water
50 cm³ sodium thiosulfate + no water

H Repeat the entire investigation again to obtain a second set of results. If time is short, your teacher may suggest that you share results with other groups instead.

AQA GCSE
Combined science
Practical 11: Rates of reaction
(Part 2: Observing a colour change)

Recording your results

1 Record your results in the table below. The final column has the concentrations of sodium thiosulfate worked out for you (providing you used the suggested amounts of water and sodium thiosulfate). This will help you with later questions.

Volume of sodium thiosulfate (cm³)	Volume of water (cm³)	Time taken for cross to disappear from view (seconds)				Concentration of sodium thiosulfate (g/dm³)
		Experiment 1	Experiment 2	Experiment 3	Mean	
10	40					8
20	30					16
30	20					24
40	10					32
50	0					40

Considering your results/conclusion

2 Draw a scatter diagram with mean time taken for cross to disappear from view (seconds) (the dependent variable) on the y-axis and sodium thiosulfate concentration (g/dm³) (the independent variable) on the x-axis. Draw a smooth curved line of best fit.

3 a Describe how concentration affects the rate of this reaction.

b Explain your answer to part **a** by referring to the shape of your diagram.

4 If the rate of reaction doubled, what would happen to the time taken for the cross to disappear?

5 Compare your results with other groups. How similar are they? Does this mean the investigation is reproducible?

6 Compare your results from Part 1 and 2. Both investigations looked at the effect of changing concentration, using different methods to measure the rate of reaction. Can you see similar pattern in both investigations?

Evaluation

7 Describe two possible sources of error in this investigation.

8 Suggest a way of reducing one of these errors.

Many inks contain a mixture of dyes. Chromatography can be used to identify inks; for example, inks from crime scenes or from documents that may have been forged. You are going to car~~ ~~ chromatography. You will then use the resul~~ ~~

Your teacher may watch to see if yo~~ ~~

- follow instructions carefully
- draw conclusions from your results.

AT links	
1	Use of appropriate apparatus to make range of measurements accurately.
4	Safe use of a range of equipment to p~~ ~~ and/or separate chemical mixtures inc~~ ~~ chromatography.

Aim

You are going to test some inks to see how many dyes they contain and calculate their R_f values.

Apparatus

- pencil and ruler
- beaker
- chromatography paper attached to a pencil, rod or splint
- two marker pens or felt-tip pens

Method

A Check that your chromatography pape~~r ~~ the bottom of the empty beaker witho~~ ~~ (as shown in the diagram).

B Take the paper out of the beaker and d~~ ~~ on the paper, about 2 cm from the bottom.

C Put a small spot of ink from each pen on your pencil line.

D Write the name of each pen or ink below each spot with a pencil.

E Pour some water into the beaker to a depth of about 1 cm.

F Lower the chromatography paper into the beaker so that the bottom of the paper is in the water, but the water level is below the spots (see the diagram).

G Leave the paper in the beaker until the water soaks up the paper and almost reaches the top of the paper. The water is the solvent for the different coloured dye compounds in each ink. The solvent is called the mobile phase in chromatography, because it is the part that moves.

H Take the paper out and immediately use a pencil to mark the location of the solvent front (the level the water has reached) before it evaporates. Leave the paper to dry.

Recording your results

1 Describe the coloured dye compounds that mixed to produce the ink in each pen.

2 Measure the distance the solvent (the water) has risen from the pencil line.

....

3 Measure the distance that each dye spot has risen from the pencil line.
Measure from the pencil line to the top of each different coloured spot.
Write your results in the tables below.

Name of pen/ink				
Colours of dye spots				
Distance of spot from pencil line (cm)				
R_f value				

Name of pen/ink				
Colours of dye spots				
Distance of spot from pencil line (cm)				
R_f value				

Considering your results/conclusions

4 Use the formula below to calculate the R_f value for each separate colour in the two inks.
Add these values to the tables above.

$$R_f = \frac{\text{distance moved by the coloured spot}}{\text{distance moved by solvent}}$$

5 Were any of the inks a pure colour? Explain your conclusion.

....

6 Did the same coloured dyes appear in more than one ink?
If so, do you think they were the same chemical compound? Explain your answer.

....

....

Evaluation

7 Why was the starting line drawn in pencil?

....

8 Why did you have to label the spots?

....

9 Why is the chromatography paper hung with the bottom just in the water?

....

Combined science

Water is one of our most valuable raw materials. It is used in washing and cleaning as well as agriculture and industry. Probably its most important use is for drinking. Around the world there is a need to ensure that water provided is fit to drink. This is known as potable water. In your investigation, you will test a sample of water before and after distilling it to see if you have managed to produce potable water.

Your teacher may watch to see if you can:
- follow instructions carefully
- work safely.

AT links		Done
2	Safe use of appropriate heating devices and techniques including use of a Bunsen burner and a water bath or electric heater.	
4	Safe use of a range of equipment to purify and/or separate chemical mixtures including evaporation, distillation.	

Method 1: Pre-distillation and post-distillation

A Obtain approximately 1 cm depth of the salty water sample and put it into a test tube.

Flame test (metal ions)

B Carry out a flame test on this sample by dipping the nichrome wire into the sample and holding it in a blue Bunsen burner flame. The flame colour will indicate which substance (positive metal ion) is present in the sample. Record your results in the table on the following page.

Possible flame colours: **yellow** – sodium, **lilac** – potassium, **crimson** – lithium, **brick red** – calcium, **green** – barium

Nitric acid/Silver nitrate test (halide ions)

C Add 3–4 drops of dilute nitric acid to the remaining salty water sample in the test tube. Then add 1 cm depth of silver nitrate solution. The colour of the precipitate will indicate which substance (negative halide ion) is present in the sample. Record your results in the table on the following page.

Possible precipitate colours: **white** – chloride ions, **cream** – bromide ions, **yellow** – iodide ions

D Clean out the test tube and move on to Method 2: Distillation.

Aim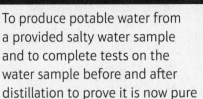

To produce potable water from a provided salty water sample and to complete tests on the water sample before and after distillation to prove it is now pure water.

Apparatus
- salty water sample
- nitric acid
- silver nitrate solution
- nichrome wire
- Bunsen burner
- heatproof mat
- test tubes

Safety ⚠
Wear eye protection.

Take care with nitric acid and silver nitrate.

Do not drink the 'pure' water.

Method 2: Distillation

E Set up your apparatus as shown in the diagram. Clamp the conical flask to the tripod and gauze. Put anti-bumping granules in the bottom of the flask.

F Adjust the Bunsen burner so that you have a gentle blue flame. The air hole should be about half open and the gas tap should be about half on. Heat the water until it boils.

G Collect the distillate in the test tube. Try to collect approximately the same amount as the original amount you tested in step **A**.

H Repeat steps **A**–**D** on this newly distilled sample of water.

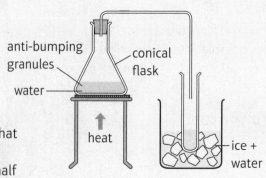

anti-bumping granules
conical flask
water
heat
ice + water

Apparatus

- salty water sample
- ice
- 250 cm³ beaker
- 250 cm³ conical flask
- clamp stand
- anti-bumping granules
- Bunsen burner
- tripod
- heatproof mat
- gauze
- delivery tube with bung

Safety ⚠️

Wear eye protection.
Tie long hair back.

Considering your results/conclusions

1 Write your results in the table below.
(Hint: Remember what results you should have obtained if using a sample of 'salty water', sodium chloride solution.)

	Sample	Flame test (positive metal ions)	Nitric acid/silver nitrate test (negative halide ions)
Before	Salty water	Yellow – Sodium	white – chloride
After	Distilled water	no colour	clear

2 Did you purify the water successfully? Explain your answer.

> Yes because we followed the method correctly. And so we added the right measurements. when we reapeted the test their will no observation or purificatios

3 What other test could you carry out to show that the newly distilled sample is water?

> Desalination Reverse osmosis can also be used to desalinate water – PH test – PH 7 – pure water Boiling point = 100°C

Evaluation

4 Explain what happened when the salty water was distilled. In your explanation, use the following words: boil, evaporate, liquid, steam, temperature, vapour. Go on to a separate sheet of paper if you need to.

> First the salty pure water was evaporating and then there was steam in the beaker. the Also the temperature was rising high. Only the pure water changed into the vapor form Vapour pass through the tube into the boiling tube. The vapor gets condensed in the boiling tube.

The specific heat capacity of a substance is the energy needed to raise the temperature of 1 kg of the substance by 1 °C. The unit of specific heat capacity is the joule per kilogram per degree Celsius (J/kg °C). You are going to calculate the specific heat capacity of a metal block and compare your findings with published results.

Your teacher may watch to see if you can:

- follow instructions carefully
- work safely.

AT links		Done
1	Use appropriate apparatus to make and record measurements of mass, time and temperature accurately.	
5	Use, in a safe manner, appropriate apparatus to measure energy changes/transfers and associated values such as work done.	

Aim
To measure the specific heat capacity of a metal block.

Apparatus

- metal block calorimeters
- insulation to wrap around the blocks
- oil
- immersion heater and power supply
- heat resistant mat
- thermometer
- stop clock
- connecting wires
- balance
- ammeter
- voltmeter

Safety ⚠

Take care as the heaters and blocks may get hot enough to burn your skin.

Hypothesis

Write down a hypothesis for this experiment.

Method

A Obtain your metal block calorimeter, make a note of the metal you have been given and measure its mass in kg.

B Put the immersion heater in the large hole and connect it as shown in the diagram to the right. Ask your teacher to check your connections.

C Put a few drops of oil in the small hole in the calorimeter. This will help to conduct energy from the block to the thermometer.

D Ensure the power supply is set to 12 V. Switch on the supply and make a note of the readings on the two meters. They should remain constant throughout the investigation.

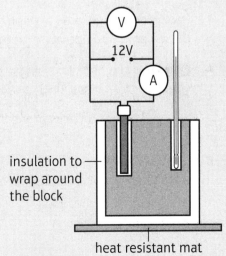

insulation to wrap around the block

heat resistant mat

E Record the temperature and start the stop clock. Record the temperature every minute for the next 10 minutes.

F The power of the immersion heater can be calculated from the current (A) that flows through it and the potential difference (V) across it. Calculate the power using the equation:

$P = I \times V$

P is the power in watts, W

I is the current in amperes (amps), A

V is the potential difference in volts, V

Block metal	Block mass (kg)	Current (A)	Potential difference (V)	Power of the heater (W)
Aliminionum	1 Ks			

Considering your results/conclusions

1 Record your results in the table below.

Time (seconds)	Temperature (°C)	Work done by the heater (J)
0	23°	0
60	23.5	1.21
120	24°C	2.40
180	25°C	3.61
240	26.5°C	4.83
300	27°C	6.04
360	28.5°C	7.24
420	29.5°C	8.44
480	30.5°C	9.65
540	31.5°C	10.8
600	32.5°C	12.0

2 To calculate the work done by the heater (the last column in your table) you will need to multiply the power value of the heater (worked out in Step **F**) by the time (in seconds).

3 On the next page, draw a graph of your results. You need to put work done by the heater on the x-axis and temperature on the y-axis. You need to add a line of best fit.

4 Find the straightest part of your graph and work out the gradient. Then use the following equation to work out the heat capacity of the block:

$\dfrac{1}{\text{gradient}}$ = heat capacity of the block

5 Use this value to calculate the specific heat capacity of the material of the block, using the following equation:

$\dfrac{\text{heat capacity of the block}}{\text{mass of the block (kg)}}$ = specific heat capacity of the block

Evaluation

6 Compare your result with the accepted published values for specific heat capacity of three different metals. How does your result compare? Explain why it might not be exactly the same.

Calorimeter block material	Specific heat capacity in joules per kilogram per degree Celsius (J/kg/°C)
Aluminium	913
Copper	385
Iron	500

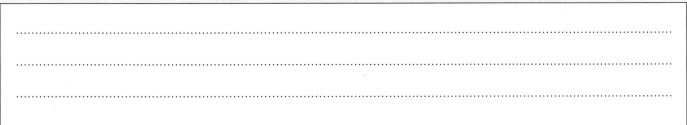

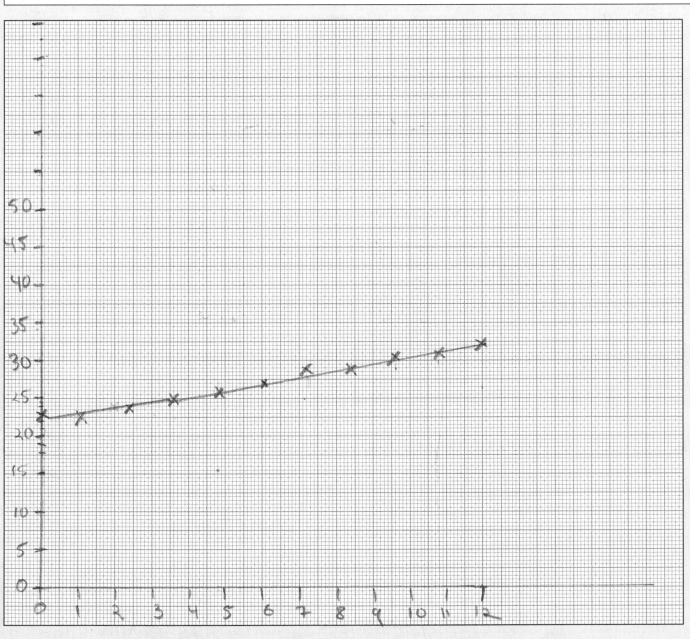

Some wires and components need a larger potential difference to produce a current through them than others. This is because they have a large electrical resistance. Resistance is measured in units called ohms (Ω). The resistance of a wire, a component or a circuit is calculated using the equation:

potential difference = current × resistance
(V)   (A)   (Ω)

First you will investigate how resistance is affected by the length of a wire. In the second experiment, you will look at resistors in series and in parallel.

Your teacher may watch to see if you can:

- follow instructions carefully
- work safely.

AT links		Done
1	Use appropriate apparatus to measure and record length accurately.	
6	Use appropriate apparatus to measure current, potential difference and resistance.	
7	Use circuit diagrams to construct and check series and parallel circuits.	

Task 1: Resistance in wires

Hypothesis

Write down a hypothesis for this experiment.

Aim

To investigate factors that affect the resistance of an electrical circuit.

Apparatus

- connecting leads
- low voltage power supply
- wire to be tested
- crocodile clips
- metre rule
- ammeter
- voltmeter

Safety

Take care as short lengths of wire can get hot. Switch off the power between readings.

Ask your teacher to check your circuit before you switch it on.

Method

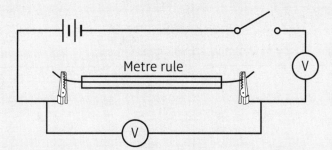

Metre rule

A Set up the circuit as shown in the diagram above. The metre rule should already have a piece of wire attached along its length. The switch which is shown in the circuit is the switch on the low voltage power supply. Set the low voltage power supply to 6 V.

B Make sure one crocodile clip is at one end of the metre rule, connected to the wire being tested.

C Clip the second crocodile clip to the wire level with the 20 cm mark. Switch on the power supply and both the meters. Record the ammeter and voltmeter readings in the table below.

D Switch off the power supply and move the second crocodile clip along the wire so a slightly longer length of wire is used. Repeat steps **A** to **D** for four more different lengths.

Considering your results/conclusions

1 Write your results in the table below.

Length of wire being tested (cm)					
Current (A)					
Potential difference (V)					
Resistance (Ω)					

2 Calculate resistance for the bottom row using the following equation:

$$\text{resistance (Ω)} = \frac{\text{potential difference (V)}}{\text{current (A)}}$$

3 On the next page, draw a graph of resistance against length of wire being tested. The resistance (dependent variable) should go on the *y*-axis and the length of wire being tested (independent variable) should go on the *x*-axis. Draw a straight line of best fit.

4 What conclusion can you draw from your results and graph?

5 Use evidence from your graph and your calculations to explain how you came to your conclusion.

Evaluation

6 a Looking at your graph, how close were your points to the line of best fit?

....

....

b What does this tell you about the quality of the data you have gathered?

....

....

7 How reproducible were your results? (Hint: Compare your results with other groups.)

....

....

Task 2: Resistors in series and parallel

Hypothesis

Write down a hypothesis for this experiment.

Method

Test 1: One resistor

A Set up the circuit as shown in the diagram on the right.

B Switch on the power supply and record the current and potential difference. Then switch off the power.

C Calculate the total resistance for the circuit using the equation:

$$\text{resistance } (\Omega) = \frac{\text{potential difference (V)}}{\text{current (A)}}$$

Current (A)	Potential difference (V)	Resistance (Ω)

Test 2: Two resistors in series

D Set up the circuit as shown in the diagram on the right.

E Switch on the power supply and record the current and potential difference. Then switch off the power.

F Calculate the total resistance for the circuit using the equation above:

Current (A)	Potential difference (V)	Resistance (Ω)

Test 3: Two resistors in parallel

G Set up the circuit as shown in the diagram on the right.

H Switch on the power supply and record the current and potential difference. Then switch off the power.

I Calculate the total resistance for the circuit using the equation above.

Current (A)	Potential difference (V)	Resistance (Ω)

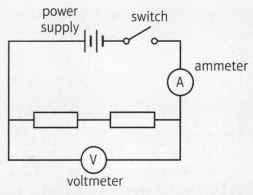

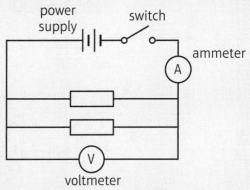

Considering your results/conclusions

1 Look at the resistance values you worked out in the three tests.
   What is the effect on the total resistance in a circuit of adding another resistor in series?
   (Hint: Compare your results for Test 1 and Test 2.)

2 What is the effect on the total resistance in a circuit of adding another resistor in parallel?
   (Hint: Compare your results for Test 1 and Test 3.)

3 What conclusions can be made about resistors in series and resistors in parallel in electrical circuits?

4 Based on your results, predict what would happen if you added:
   a a third resistor in series

   b a third resistor in parallel?

A diode has a low resistance if the potential difference is in one direction but a very high resistance if the potential difference is in the opposite direction. This means that current can only flow in one direction. A light-dependent resistor (LDR) has a high resistance in the dark but the resistance decreases as the light intensity increases. A thermistor has a high resistance at low temperatures but as the temperature increases the resistance decreases. You will investigate these three devices and produce a graph of current (A) against potential difference (V) for each one.

Your teacher may watch to see if you can:

- follow instructions carefully
- work safely.

AT links		Done
6	Use appropriate apparatus to measure current and potential difference and to explore the characteristics of a variety of circuit elements.	
7	Use circuit diagrams to construct and check series and parallel circuits including a variety of common circuit elements.	

Aim

To investigate what happens to the current through three different components (resistor, diode and filament lamp) when the p.d across them changes.

Apparatus

- connecting leads
- low voltage power supply
- resistor
- ammeter
- voltmeter
- variable resistor

Safety

Ask your teacher to check your circuit before you switch it on.

Task 1: Resistor

Hypothesis

Write down a hypothesis for this experiment. This hypothesis could include a sketch graph.

Method

A If the low voltage power supply allows you to vary the potential difference, there is no need to use a variable resistor. Your teacher will explain this to you.

B Set up the circuit as shown in the diagram below. Ensure that, when the circuit is switched on, both the ammeter and voltmeter have *positive* readings. If either meter has a negative value, swap over the connecting leads on the terminals going into the meter.

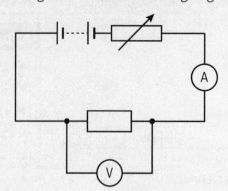

C Draw a suitable table in the space provided on page 59 and record the current and potential difference.

D Adjust the variable resistor or low voltage supply and record the new current and potential difference readings.

E Repeat step **D**.

F Switch off the circuit and swap over the connections going into the power supply.

G Ensure that when you switch on the circuit this time, there are negative readings on both meters.

H Repeat steps **C–E**.

Task 2: Filament lamp

Hypothesis

Write down a hypothesis for this experiment. This hypothesis could include a sketch graph.

Method

A If the low voltage power supply allows you to vary potential difference, there is no need to use a variable resistor. Your teacher will explain this to you.

B Set up the circuit as shown in the diagram below. Ensure that, when the circuit is switched on, both the ammeter and voltmeter have *positive* readings. If either meter has a negative value, swap over the connecting leads on the terminals going into the meter.

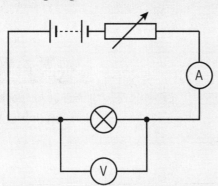

C Draw a suitable table in the space provided on page 59 and record the current and potential difference.

D Adjust the variable resistor or low voltage supply and record the new current and potential difference readings.

E Repeat step **D**.

F Switch off the circuit and swap over the connections going into the power supply.

G Ensure that when you switch on the circuit this time, there are negative readings on both meters.

H Repeat steps **C–E**.

Task 3: Diode

Hypothesis

Write down a hypothesis for this experiment. This hypothesis could include a sketch graph.

Method

A If the low voltage power supply allows you to vary the potential difference, there is no need to use a variable resistor. Your teacher will explain this to you.

B Set up the circuit as show in the diagram below. It looks similar to the previous experiments but has a couple of changes. The diode must be protected with a protective resistor to stop the current through it becoming too large. The ammeter will need to be replaced with a milliammeter due to the low currents flowing through it. Do not alter the potential difference to make it greater than 6 V.

 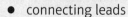
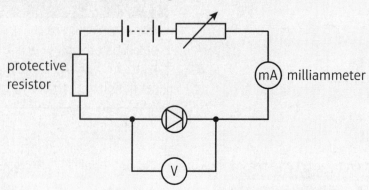

C Ensure that, when the circuit is switched on, both the ammeter and voltmeter have *positive* readings. If either meter has a negative value, swap over the connecting leads on the terminals going into the meter.

D Draw a suitable table in the space provided below and record the new current and potential difference.

E Adjust the variable resistor or low voltage supply and record new current and potential difference readings.

F Repeat step **E**.

G Switch off the circuit and swap over the connections going into the power supply.

H Ensure that when you switch on the circuit this time, there are negative readings on both meters.

I Repeat steps **D–F**.

Considering your results/conclusions

1 Use the space below to record the results from your three experiments. Continue on a separate piece of paper if necessary. You should have four to five readings for each component. If you did not complete all the investigations yourself, obtain results from other groups.

2 Draw a graph for the resistor. Current (the dependent variable) should go on the *y*-axis and potential difference (the independent variable) should go on the *x*-axis. You will have negative values so the origin (at 0 V, 0 A) will be in the middle of the graph paper. If you are unsure, ask your teacher about the likely shape. Draw a line of best fit through your points. It should be a straight line passing through the origin (i.e. at 0 V the current should be 0 A).

3 Draw a graph for the filament lamp. Current (the dependent variable) should go on the y-axis and potential difference (the independent variable) should go on the x-axis. You will have negative values so the origin (at 0 V, 0 A) will be in the middle of the graph paper. If you are unsure, ask your teacher about the likely shape. Draw a curved line of best fit through your points. The line is sometimes described as an S-shape and must go through the origin (i.e. at 0 V the current should be 0 A).

4   Draw a graph for the diode. Current (the dependent variable) should go on the *y*-axis and potential difference (the independent variable) should go on the *x*-axis . This time, however, you should not have any negative values for current so the *x*-axis will sit at the bottom of your graph paper. There will still be negative values for potential difference so the *y*-axis should be in the middle of your paper. If you are unsure, ask your teacher about the likely shape. Draw a line of best fit through your points.

5 Use your results to describe the relationship between potential difference, current and resistance for:

a a resistor

b a filament lamp

c a diode.

Evaluation

6 Describe how you tried to ensure the measurements you recorded were as accurate as possible.

7 Describe what you could do to make your investigation more accurate.

8 Look at a textbook or website and find some published current–potential difference (I–V) graphs for a resistor, a filament lamp and a diode. Do the shape of your graphs match the examples you found?
Explain your answer.

The density of a substance is the mass of a certain volume of that substance. Almost all substances are most dense when they are solid and least dense when they are gas. The arrangement of particles can explain the differences in density between different states of matter. A solid is usually denser than the same substance as a liquid, because the particles in solids are closer together.

You will complete three experiments on density. You will determine the density of irregular shaped objects, regular shaped objects and liquids.

Your teacher may watch to see if you can:

- follow instructions carefully
- work safely.

AT links		Done
1	Use appropriate apparatus to make and record measurements of length, area, mass and volume accurately. Use such measurements to determine the density of solid objects and liquids.	

Task 1: Density of regular shaped objects

Hypothesis

Write down a hypothesis for this experiment.

Aim

To identify a substance from its density.

Apparatus

- balance
- regular shaped objects/ blocks
- ruler

Method

A Select four different regular shaped objects from the selection provided. If they have labels, write these in the first column. Otherwise write a brief description (e.g. black cube).

B Measure all the dimensions (i.e. length, width and height) for each object in centimetres to one decimal place. Record your results in the table below.

C Measure the mass of each object in grams and record this in the table below.

Recording your results

1 To calculate volume (column **6**), multiply length (column **2**) by width (column **3**) by height (column **4**).

2 To calculate density (column **7**), use the equation:

$$\text{density (g/cm}^3\text{)} = \frac{\text{mass (g)}}{\text{volume (cm}^3\text{)}}$$

1	2	3	4	5	6	7	8
Object	Length (cm)	Width (cm)	Height (cm)	Mass (g)	Volume (cm³)	Density (g/cm³)	Material substance is made from

3 Use the table below to work out what each substance is and complete column **8**.

Substance	Aluminium	Brass	Copper	Iron	Lead	Wood	Zinc
Density in g/cm³	2.70	8.55	8.92	7.80	11.34	0.71	7.14

4 Ask your teacher for the correct answers for each material. How well did you do?

....

....

Your teacher may watch to see if you can:

- take careful measurements.

Task 2: Densities of irregular shaped objects

Method

A Choose an irregular shaped object from the selection provided and measure its mass. Write the name of the material and the mass of the object in the table below. Tie some thread or very thin string around the object.

B Stand a displacement can on the bench with its spout over a bowl. Fill the can with water until the water just starts to come out of the spout.

C Hold a measuring cylinder under the spout and carefully lower the object into the can using the string.

D If your object floats, carefully push it down until all of it is under the water. Your finger should not be in the water.

E Stand the measuring cylinder on the bench and read the volume of water you have collected. This is the same as the volume of your object. Record this volume in the table below.

F Repeat steps **A**–**E** with four more irregular shaped objects.

Aim

To compare the densities of different liquids and solids.

Apparatus

- balance
- displacement can
- measuring cylinder
- bowl
- solids
- irregular shaped objects for testing
- thread or very thin string

Safety ⚠️

Mop up any spills straight away.

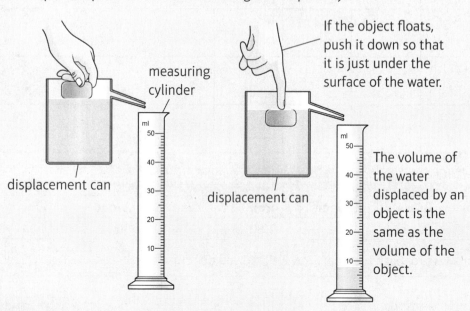

measuring cylinder

displacement can

If the object floats, push it down so that it is just under the surface of the water.

displacement can

The volume of the water displaced by an object is the same as the volume of the object.

Recording your results

1 Complete the table below.

Material	Mass (g)	Volume (cm³)	Density (g/cm³)

2 Calculate the density of each solid and write it in the table. The equation you need is:

$$\text{density (g/cm}^3) = \frac{\text{mass (g)}}{\text{volume (cm}^3)}$$

Task 3: Densities of liquids

Method

A Put an empty beaker on a balance and zero the balance.

B Use a measuring cylinder to measure 50 cm³ of a liquid and pour it into the beaker. Write down the name of the liquid and the reading on the balance. This is the mass of 50 cm³ of the liquid.

C Repeat step **B** with four more liquids.

Apparatus

- balance
- measuring cylinder
- beaker
- liquids

Safety ⚠

Mop up any spills straight away.

Recording your results

1 Complete the table below.

Liquid	Mass of 50 cm³ (g)	Density (g/cm³)

2 Calculate the density of each liquid and write it in the table. The equation you need is:

$$\text{density (g/cm}^3) = \frac{\text{mass (g)}}{\text{volume (cm}^3)}$$

Considering your results/conclusions

3 **a** What was the range of densities for the solids you measured?

....

....

b What was the range of densities for the liquids?

....

....

4 Compare the densities of the solids and liquids that you tested.

....

....

....

Designers need to know the characteristics of springs so that they can choose the best spring for their purpose. The extension of a spring (or other object) is the change in length when forces are applied. You will investigate this relationship by applying weights to a spring and measuring the extension. You will use the information to calculate work done to stretch the spring.

Your teacher may watch to see if you can:

- take careful measurements.

AT links		Done
1	Use appropriate apparatus to make and record length accurately.	
2	Use appropriate apparatus to measure and observe the effect of force on the extension of springs and collect the data required to plot a force-extension graph.	

Aim

To investigate the extension and work done when applying forces to a spring.

Apparatus

- stand and two clamps
- springs
- ruler
- masses
- eye protection

Safety ⚠

Wear eye protection.

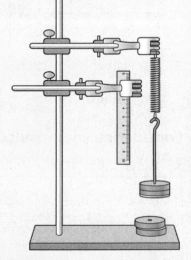

Method

A Set up the apparatus as shown in the diagram. The zero on the ruler should be level with the bottom of the unstretched spring.

B Measure the length of the spring with no masses hanging on it and write it down.

C Hang a 100 g mass on the spring. Record the extension of the spring (the length shown on the ruler).

D Repeat step **C** until you have found the extension of the spring with 10 different masses. Each 100 g mass puts a downwards force of 1 N on the spring.

E Repeat steps **A**–**D** for a different spring.

Recording your results

1 Draw a table like this to record your results.

	Spring 1		Spring 2	
Force (N)	Extension (cm)	Extension (m)	Extension (cm)	Extension (m)
0	0	0		
1				

2 Draw a scatter diagram to show force in newtons against extension in metres.
   Put extension on the horizontal axis and force on the vertical axis. Plot points for all your
   springs on the same diagram and join them with lines of best fit.

Considering your results/conclusions

3 Which of your springs feel the stiffest? (Which ones take more force to pull them?)

4 Calculate the gradient of the line on your diagram for each spring. The gradient gives you the
   spring constant for each spring. The spring constant gives a measure of how stiff a spring is:
   the larger the spring constant, the stiffer the spring.

5 How can you work out which springs should feel the stiffest by looking at their spring constants?

....

....

....

....

....

....

6 The work done to stretch a spring can be calculated using the following equation:

energy transferred in stretching (J) = $\frac{1}{2}$ × spring constant (N/m) × extension^2 (m)^2

Calculate the energy transferred in stretching each of the springs that you tested.

....

In drag racing, the aim is to get to the end of a straight track as quickly as possible. The most important feature of the bike is its acceleration. Drag racers try to improve the performance of their bikes by changing the force produced by the engine and the tyres, or by changing the mass of the bike. In this practical, you are going to use trolleys as a model of a motorbike to investigate the effects of mass and force on acceleration.

Your teacher may watch to see if you can:
- follow instructions safely
- take careful measurements.

AT links		Done
1	Use appropriate apparatus to make and record measurements of length, mass and time accurately.	
2	Use appropriate apparatus to measure and observe the effect of force.	
3	Use appropriate apparatus and techniques to measure motion, including determination of speed and rate of change of speed (acceleration/deceleration).	

Part 1: Effect of mass
Method
A Prop up one end of the ramp and place a trolley on it. Adjust the slope of the ramp until the trolley just starts to move on its own. The force of gravity pulling the trolley down the slope is now slightly greater than the friction between the trolley's wheels and the ramp.

B Stick a piece of card to the top of the trolley using sticky putty. Leave enough space to stack some masses on top of the trolley. Measure the length of the card and write it down.

C Find the mass of the trolley and write it down.

D Fasten the pulley at the bottom end of the ramp, and arrange the string and masses as shown in the diagram.

Aim

To investigate the effect of mass on the acceleration of a trolley.

Apparatus

- trolley
- ramp
- blocks to prop up the end of the ramp
- string
- pulley
- masses
- sticky tape
- card
- sticky putty
- balance
- two light gates
- datalogger
- two clamps and stands
- box of crumpled newspaper

Safety ⚠️

Make sure masses cannot fall on your feet by placing a box of crumpled newspaper on the floor beneath them.

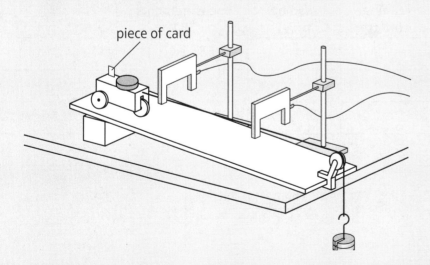
piece of card

E Set up two light gates, one near the top of the ramp and one near the bottom. Adjust their positions so that the card on the top of the trolley passes through both gates as it runs down the ramp.

F Put a mass on the end of the string. You will keep this mass the same for all your tests. You will have to decide what mass to use.

G Release the trolley from the top of the ramp and write down the speed of the trolley (from the datalogger) as it passes through *each* light gate. Also write down the time it takes for the trolley to travel from one light gate to the other.

H Repeat step **G** adding other masses to the trolley (Keep the same mass on the string.) You will have to decide what masses to use, how many different masses to test, and whether you need to repeat any of your tests.

Prediction

1 You will accelerate a trolley using a constant force. What effect do you think the mass of the trolley will have on the acceleration? Explain your prediction if you can. Record your prediction and ideas in the box below.

Recording your results

2 Record your results in the table below.

Mass added to trolley (kg)	Total mass of trolley and masses (kg)	Run number	u – 1st velocity reading (m/s)	v – 2nd velocity reading (m/s)	Time between velocity measurements (s)	Acceleration (m/s²)
		1				
		2				
		3				
		Mean				

3 Calculate the acceleration for each run using the formula in the box.

4 Find the mean acceleration for each trolley mass.

$$\text{acceleration} = \frac{\text{change in velocity}}{\text{time}}$$

$$a = \frac{(v - u)}{t}$$

Considering your results

5 Plot a scatter graph to show your results. Put the total mass of the trolley (the independent variable) on the *x*-axis and the acceleration (the dependent variable) on the *y*-axis, as shown in the diagram. Draw a line or curve of best fit through your points.

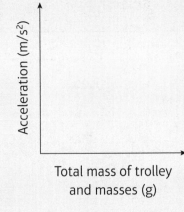

6 a What relationship between acceleration and mass does your graph show?

....

....

....

....

b Is this what you predicted?

....

....

....

....

Evaluation

7 **a** How close are the points on your graph to the line of best fit?

....
....
....
....
....
....

b What does this tell you about the quality of the data you have gathered?

....
....
....
....
....
....

8 How do your results compare with the results obtained by other groups?

....
....
....
....
....
....

9 How certain are you that your conclusion is correct? Explain your answer.

....
....
....
....
....
....

Part 2: Effect of force
Method

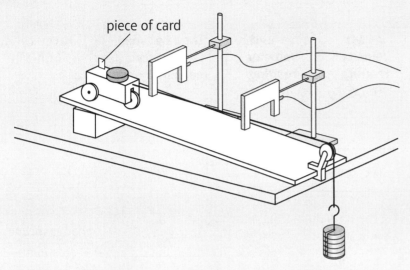

piece of card

Aim

To investigate the effect of force on the acceleration of a trolley.

Apparatus

- trolley
- ramp
- blocks to prop up the end of the ramp
- string
- pulley
- masses
- sticky tape
- card
- sticky putty
- balance
- two light gates
- datalogger
- two clamps and stands
- box of crumpled newspaper

A Set up the experiment as for part 1. The diagram above will help you.

B Add five weights or masses to the mass holder on the string.

C Release the trolley from the top of the ramp and write down the speed of the trolley (from the datalogger) as it passes through *each* light gate. Also write down the time it takes for the trolley to travel from one light gate to the other.

D Remove one mass and place it on top of the trolley. This will keep the total mass constant. Don't forget that the mass stack is also being accelerated! Repeat step **C**.

E Repeat steps **C** and **D** for each further mass. Each time, place the mass removed from the mass holder on top of the trolley.

Safety

Make sure masses cannot fall on your feet by placing a box of crumpled newspaper on the floor beneath them.

Prediction

1 The trolley will be a constant mass. What effect do you think altering the force applied will have on the acceleration? Explain your prediction if you can. Record your prediction and ideas in the box below.

Recording your results

2 Record your results in the table below. The total mass of the trolley and masses should be the same for each experiment.

Force (N)	Total mass of trolley and masses (kg)	Run number	u – 1st velocity reading (m/s)	v – 2nd velocity reading (m/s)	Time between velocity measurements (s)	Acceleration (m/s²)
		1				
		2				
		3				
		Mean				

3 Calculate the acceleration for each run using the formula in the box.

4 Find the mean acceleration for each force.

Considering your results

5 Plot a scatter graph to show your results. Put the force in newtons (the independent variable) on the x-axis and the acceleration (the dependent variable) on the y-axis, as shown in the diagram. Draw a line or curve of best fit through your points.

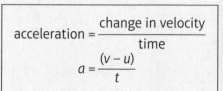

$$\text{acceleration} = \frac{\text{change in velocity}}{\text{time}}$$

$$a = \frac{(v - u)}{t}$$

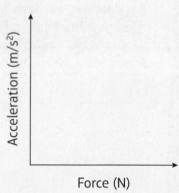

Acceleration (m/s²)

Force (N)

6 a What relationship between acceleration and force does your graph show?

b Is this what you predicted?

Evaluation

7 a How close are the points on your graph to the line of best fit?

b What does this tell you about the quality of the data you have gathered?

8 How do your results compare with the results obtained by other groups?

9 How certain are you that your conclusion is correct? Explain your answer.

Light waves do not travel very far through sea water before being absorbed by the water or reflected by tiny particles in the water. This makes it impossible to take pictures of things that are deep down on the sea bed. Scientists and explorers use sonar equipment to send sound waves into the water and detect echoes. The depth can be worked out from the speed of sound in the water and the time it takes for the echo to return. The speed, frequency and wavelength of waves can be measured in different ways. The most suitable equipment for making these measurements depends on the type of wave and on its speed. You are going to use different pieces of equipment to measure the speed and wavelength of waves on the surface of water, and the speed and frequency of sound waves in solids.

Aim

To measure the speed and frequency of waves on the surface of water and evaluate the suitability of the equipment.

Apparatus

- ripple tank
- stopwatch
- ruler
- digital camera

Safety ⚠️

Mop up any spilled water straight away.

Your teacher may watch to see if you can:

- follow instructions carefully
- make accurate measurements.

AT links		Done
4	Make observations of waves in fluids and solids to identify the suitability of apparatus to measure speed, frequency and wavelength.	

Part 1: Speed of waves on water

Method

A   Set up a ripple tank with a straight dipper close to one of the short sides of the tank. Fasten a ruler to one of the long sides so you can see the markings above the water level.

B   Vary the current to the motor until you get waves with a wavelength about half as long as the ripple tank (so you can always see two waves).

C   Count how many waves are formed in 10 seconds and record this number in the space on the next page.

D   Look at the waves against the ruler. Use the markings on the ruler to estimate the wavelength of the waves. If you have a camera, use it to take a photo of the waves with a ruler held just above them. Record your estimated wavelength in the space on the next page.

E   Mark two points on the edge of the ripple tank and measure the distance between them. Use the stopwatch to find out how long it takes a wave to travel from one mark to the other. Record this value in the space on the next page.

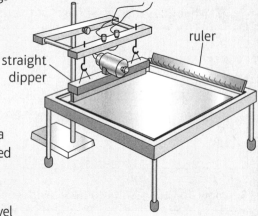
straight dipper
ruler

Recording your results

Number of waves counted [Step C]:

Estimated wavelength [Step D]:

Distance between two points [Step E]:

Time taken for wave to travel between two points [Step E]:

Using your results

1   Calculate the speed of a single wave by dividing the distance by the time (both from step **E**).
    Make sure your distance is in metres and your time is in seconds.

....

2   Find the frequency by taking the number of waves in 10 seconds (from step **C**) and dividing
    by 10. Then calculate the speed of the series of waves by multiplying the wavelength (from
    step **D**) by the frequency you have just worked out.

....

Considering your results/conclusions

3   Compare your results from questions **1** and **2** with the results obtained by other groups.
    Are your results similar? If not, can you explain the differences?

....

....

....

Evaluation

4   How easy was it to measure the frequency in step **C**? Why did you count the number of
    waves in 10 seconds?

....

....

....

5   How easy was it to measure the wavelength in step **D**? It was suggested that you use a
    camera to help you do this. What is the benefit of doing this?

....

....

....

6   How easy was it to time a single wave in step **E**? Is there any way you could improve this
    measurement?

....

....

....

Part 2: Measuring waves in a solid

Method

A Suspend a metal rod horizontally using clamp stands and rubber bands, as shown in the diagram below.

B Hit one end of the rod with a hammer. Hold a smartphone with a frequency app close to the rod and note down the peak frequency.

C Measure the length of the rod and write it down. The wavelength will be twice the length of the rod. Record the wavelength in the space below.

Aim

To measure the speed and frequency of sound waves in solids and evaluate the suitability of the equipment.

Apparatus

- metre rule
- hammer
- two clamps and stands
- long metal rod
- rubber bands
- smartphone with frequency app

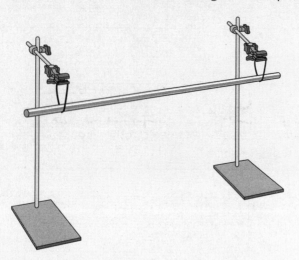

Recording your results

Frequency [step **B**]:

Wavelength [step **C**]:

1 Use the frequency (from step **B**) and the wavelength (from step **C**) to calculate the speed of sound in the metal rod.

Considering your results/conclusions

2 What is the speed of sound in the material you tested?

....

....

Evaluation

3 Explain which of your measurements is more accurate: the wavelength or the frequency.

....

....

....

....

4 Complete the table below to summarise the equipment you used for the measurements in both parts of this investigation. Assess how suitable the equipment was.

What was measured?	Which material was this measured for?	How was it measured?	Why was this method chosen?

5 You can measure walking speed using a tape measure and a stop clock. Explain why these instruments are not suitable for measuring the speed of sound in a solid.

....

....

....

....

....

A radiator in a car is designed to transfer energy to the outside air, to stop the engine overheating. Radiators to cool car engines were patented over 100 years ago, in 1879. Radiators are often painted to help them to transfer more energy by radiation. Different types of surface affect how much energy is transferred by radiation from different objects. You will investigate the effect of different coloured surfaces on the amount of energy transferred by radiation from a tube of hot water.

Your teacher may watch to see if you can:

- take careful measurements
- present your results as a line graph.

AT links		Done
1	Use appropriate apparatus to make and record temperature accurately.	
4	Make observations of the effects of the interaction of electromagnetic waves with matter.	

Method

A Cover four boiling tubes in different coloured materials. Try to use the same type of material (e.g. paper) and the same thickness for each tube. Fasten the materials in place with sticky tape.

B Use the measuring cylinder to pour the same volume of hot water from a kettle into each tube.

C Measure the temperature of the water in each tube and start the stop clock.

D Record the temperature of the water in each tube every two minutes for 20 minutes.

Recording your results

1 Record your results in the table below.

Time (min)	Temperature (°C)			
	Tube 1 white	Tube 2 yellow	Tube 3 black	Tube 4 Red
0	58° 56°	55°	·60°	53°
2	54°	52°	57°	50°
4	51°	48°	54°	46°
6	49	45	51	45
8	47	43	49	43°
10	45	41	47	42
12	43	40	45	41
14	43	39	43	39
16	43 42	38°	42	41
18	40	38	40	37°
20	38	36	39°	36°
change in temperature	18	19	41	17

Apparatus

- four boiling tubes
- test tube rack
- measuring cylinder
- four thermometers
- stop clock
- insulating materials
- sticky tape
- hot water

Safety

Take care with hot water.

2 Draw a line graph to present your results. Time (the independent variable) go on the *x*-axis and temperature (the dependent variable) should go on the *y*-axis. Plot all four sets of results on the same axes and join each set of points with a smooth curve of best fit.

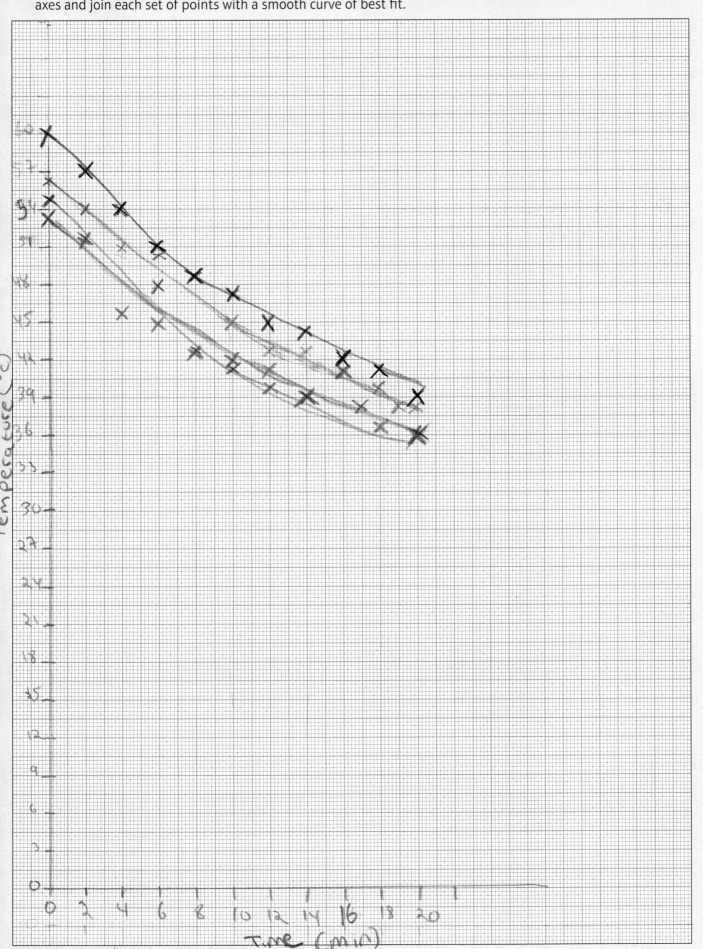

Considering your results/conclusions

3 Describe what your graph shows about the rate of cooling of the water in each tube.

AS

4 Which colour is best at emitting radiation? Which is the worst? Explain your conclusion.

Black is best at emitting radiation because its temperature change is the highest. The worst at emitting radiation is white because its temperature change is the lowest.

Evaluation

5 How well do your results support your conclusion? Your answer should refer to your graph.

6 Can you draw a general conclusion from your results (such as that light colours emit more radiation than dark colours)? Explain your answer.

Combined science

1 Microscopy

Drawings for Methods 1, 2 and 3

Cells should be drawn with a sharp pencil and clean lines. Labels should be drawn with a ruler and should not overlap. Your writing should be neat. The magnification or scale should be added to show the size of the cells.

2 Osmosis

1–7 Your own answers.

8 The potato slices that gained mass did so because water moved by osmosis into the root from the surrounding solution. The potato slices that lost mass did so because water moved by osmosis from the root into the surrounding solution. Any potato slices that didn't change mass would have been in a solution with the same solute concentration as the potato cells.

9 Percentage change removes any variation due to differences in initial mass between slices.

10 Calculating a mean takes away or reduces the impact of any possible anomalous results which could be caused by variations between the potatoes.

11 Your own suggestion.

3 Food tests

1 Your results will depend on the food supplied and tested. The table shows some typical results.

Food	Iodine test	Benedict's test	Biuret test	Emulsion test
full-fat milk	yellow–orange	yellow	purple	cloudy
whey	yellow–orange	bright blue	purple	clear
egg white	yellow–orange	bright blue	purple	clear
potato	black–blue	bright blue	light blue	clear
glucose	yellow–orange	red precipitate	light blue	clear
(icing sugar)	yellow–orange	bright blue	light blue	clear

2 Your answers will depend on the foods supplied and tested.

3 This will depend on the results obtained if they were not as expected. Errors are most likely to occur if equipment is not cleaned properly between tests and food becomes contaminated with another sample. Therefore, it would be a good idea to ensure equipment (i.e. glassware, spatulas etc.) is cleaned between tests. Using coloured foods may make some colour changes more difficult to see. To overcome this problem, select foods that have neutral or muted colours.

4 Enzymes

1–10 Your own results.

5 Photosynthesis

1–4 Your own results.

5 🛈 Light intensity varies with distance according to the inverse square law. So, if you double the distance from

the light source (move the lamp away), the light intensity is $\frac{1}{2^2}$ or $\frac{1}{4}$ times the original intensity (it reduces to a quarter of the original value). If you halve the distance to the light source (move the lamp closer), light intensity is $\frac{1}{\left(\frac{1}{2}\right)^2}$ which

is 4 times the original. This is the pattern you should see in the graph. Take a measurement in the middle of your values and look at what happens when that result is doubled or halved to see if it fits the inverse square law.

6 To show that light is required for the algal balls to photosynthesise. No colour change should have occurred in the control bottle, proving that light is required by the algal balls.

6 Reaction time

1 This is likely to be a bar chart. The dependent variable (the results) should be on the *y*-axis and the independent variable (the students taking part in the experiment) should be on the *x*-axis.

2 **a** Your own answer.

b There could be a correlation between fast reaction times and skill at reaction sports (basketball, football, hockey or tennis for example). The same is somewhat true for video games but this does depend on the style of game being played.

3 Your results are likely to improve as you practise more and learn what to expect. But they will also plateau. You can only get so quick on this test without resorting to cheating (e.g. anticipating and closing your hand before the ruler is dropped).

4 Some possible ways to improve the experiment include: increasing the number of repeats to ten drops per person, changing the hand to see if there is a difference with the other hand, altering the dropping point of the ruler.

5 Use a computer program or app where you have to press a button when a light or image is displayed. This would collect all of the data and ensure that reaction times are correctly measured.

7 Field investigations

1–7 Your own results.

8 Making salts

1 The crystals are blue and diamond shaped. (The size will vary depending on conditions.)

2 **a** clear solution

b black solid (powder)

c blue solution

3 copper oxide + sulfuric acid → copper sulfate + water

4 So that all the acid is used up.

5 copper oxide

6 copper sulfate

7 This is known as a neutralisation reaction because the hydrogen ions of the acid are removed (and a salt and water are formed). The hydrogen ions make the initial solution acidic whereas the final solution is neutral as both the salt and water are neutral substances.

8 copper oxide

9 $CuO(s) + H_2SO_4(aq) \rightarrow CuSO_4(aq) + H_2O(l)$

9 Electrolysis

1

Solution	Positive electrode	Negative electrode	Evidence for this...
copper (II) chloride	chlorine	copper	(positive electrode) bubbling at electrode which bleaches damp litmus paper
			(negative electrode) brown/pink substance on electrode
copper (II) sulfate	oxygen	copper	(positive electrode) bubbling at electrode (which doesn't bleach litmus paper)
			(negative electrode) brown/pink substance on electrode

sodium chloride	chlorine	hydrogen	(positive electrode) bubbling at electrode which doesn't bleach damp litmus paper
			(negative electrode) bubbling at electrode (which bleaches damp litmus paper)
sodium sulfate	oxygen	hydrogen	(positive electrode) bubbling at electrode (which doesn't bleaches damp litmus paper)
			(negative electrode) bubbling at electrode (which doesn't bleaches damp litmus paper)

2   Your own comparisons.

3   Hydrogen gas: use lit wooden splint/spill, it should go out with a pop.

Oxygen gas: use a glowing wooden splint/spill, it should relight.

10 Temperature changes

1–3   Your own results.

4   This should be the volume of sodium hydroxide at the point where the lines of best fit cross. The hydrochloric acid will be 30 cm^3 (as this is the initial volume and doesn't change).

5   At this point, no reaction is taking place. The acid is used up and sodium hydroxide is now in excess. It is this excess, colder, sodium hydroxide which lowers the temperature.

6   Use a digital temperature sensor so the reading can more easily be seen going up and down. (It would also have the benefit of increasing precision.)

7   Select the region where the lines of best fit cross and read off the sodium hydroxide volume from the graph. Using this value as a guide, repeat the investigation but add 1 cm^3 volumes which are approximately 5 cm^3 either side of the sodium hydroxide value recorded as the maximum.

11 Rates of reaction

Part 1

1   Your own results.

2   If results are good, the scatter diagram should show two curves rising steadily and levelling off at about the same point. The curve for the higher concentration of acid should rise and level off more quickly.

3   The scatter diagram for both experiments should level off and become horizontal.

4   Increasing the concentration increases the rate of the reaction (makes the reaction faster).

5   The higher acid concentration (2.0 mol/dm^3) should have produced a larger amount of gas in a shorter time, so the line drawn on the graph relating to these results should have been steeper at the start.

6   Possible sources of error are: measuring the volume of gas (which is difficult because of the bubbles in the measuring cylinder) and making sure the marble chips are all the same size, otherwise their surface area could have an impact on reaction rate. (Other answers are possible.)

7   Measure the volume of gas produced for a longer time, or measure larger volumes of gas. (Other answers are possible.)

Part 2

1   Your own results.

2   The scatter diagram should show a curve, but starting off high on the left (low concentration of sodium thiosulfate) and decreasing to the bottom right (high concentration of sodium thiosulfate).

3   **a**   The rate increases quickly as the concentration of sodium thiosulfate increases.

   b   The scatter diagram shows that as the concentration increases, the time for the reaction decreases; this means the rate of reaction increases.

4   The time taken would halve.

5   Your own view, depending on other results.

6   Both experiments should show that increasing the concentration increases the rate of a reaction.

7   Any of the following measurements: time and volume of solutions.

8   Errors with recording time could be reduced by repeating the experiment more times. Errors with measuring volume of solution could be reduced by using burettes and/or pipettes. (Other answers are possible.)

12 Chromatography

1   You should have correctly identified different colours in the inks you tested.

2   You should have correctly measured from the pencil line to where the solvent reached.

3   Your own results.

4   Your own results.

5   This is dependent on your results; you need to look for any black inks which did not separate into a number of colours – the ink just remained as one main dot. Remember, the inks must have moved otherwise they would be insoluble in water.

6   Again, this is dependent on your results. However, similar coloured dyes (in the same location) on your chromatography paper are likely to contain the same chemical compound.

7   The graphite from the pencil will not dissolve in the solvent (water) and so will not interfere with the results. This will also help when working out the R_f values, as there will be a clear point from which to take measurements.

8   This was done so you could easily recall which pen/original colour of ink was used to produce each spot of ink.

9   So the water rises up the paper, and dissolves the dyes.

13 Water purification

1   Likely answers would be:

	Sample	Flame test (positive metal ions)	Nitric acid/silver nitrate test (negative halide ions)
Before	Salty water	yellow indicating sodium (ions) present	white indicating chloride (ions) present
After	Distilled water	no colour change visible (various metal ions not present)	remains clear (so no halide ions present)

2   Your own answer and explanation.

3   Add the sample to white anhydrous copper(II) sulfate and it will turn blue, or blue cobalt(II) chloride paper will turn pink. Remember that these tests do not tell you if the water is pure: they can only tell you if the sample contains water.

4   Your answer should include:

   liquid is heated until it boils; liquid/water evaporates and turns into steam, also known as water vapour; steam is pure water vapour; the steam/vapour passes into the condenser, where it cools down; when it cools it turns from a vapour/gas back into a liquid; the pure water collects as the distillate; anything dissolved in the water should remain in the conical flask.

14 Specific heat capacity

1–5 Your own results.

6 There are various explanations for the experimental results not being the same as published values. Discounting any errors made during the calculation stage (e.g. working out the correct gradient or plotting points correctly), there are other parts of the investigation that increase the chance of deviation. These include:

- difficulty reading the thermometer at the start (often it is below the level of the block and needs to be raised so it can be read)
- difficulty reading fluctuating ammeter and voltmeter readings; this will result in an inaccurate power value for the heater.

15 Resistance

Task 1: Resistance in wires

1–3 Your own results.

4 As the length of the wire increases, so does the resistance.

5 Your own explanation.

6 a Your own answer.

   b The closer the points are to the line of best fit, the better the quality of the data you have gathered.

7 Your own conclusion.

Task 2: Resistors in series and parallel

1 The total resistance of the circuit has increased.

2 The total resistance of the circuit is less than the resistance of the individual resistors.

3 Adding more resistors in series **increases** the total resistance in the circuit because the current through the resistors is **reduced** but the total potential difference across them remains the **same**. Adding more resistors in parallel **decreases** the total resistance because the total current through the resistors is increased but the total potential difference across them is **unchanged**.

4 a Total resistance would increase.

   b Total resistance would decrease.

16 Current–voltage characteristics

1–4 Your own results.

5 a As potential difference changes, the current changes by the same percentage. The graph is a straight line going through the origin because the resistance stays the same.

   b A potential difference across a filament lamp causes a current to flow through it. The current causes the filament to heat up and glow. The greater the potential difference, the more current flows and the hotter the filament becomes. As the filament heats up, its resistance increases. This means that when the potential difference changes, the current does not change by the same percentage (the two variables are not in direction proportion). The graph starts to plateau at either end.

   c A diode has a low resistance if the potential difference is in one direction but a very high resistance if the potential difference is in the opposite direction. This means current can only flow in one direction. The resistance is usually high at negative and very small potential differences, but a diode behaves like a resistor above a certain positive potential difference.

6 Possible answers include:

- check for zero error on ammeter and voltmeter
- prevent components heating up by switching off the power when not recording values.

7 Possible answers include:

- take multiple readings and work out a mean
- use a datalogger to take readings and at multiple potential differences and generate a graph.

8 Your own comparisons and explanation.

17 Density

Task 1

1–4 Your own results.

Task 2

1–2 Your own results.

Task 3

1–2 Your own results.

3 Your own results. The range of densities for the solids tested is likely to have been greater than the range of densities for the liquids.

4 The answer depends on the materials tested. You could point out that, in general, solids are more dense than liquids, although there are some solids that are less dense. Very good answers may also suggest whether each solid will float or sink in the different liquids tested.

18 Force and extension

1 Your own results.

2 Your own scatter diagram.

3 Answer will depend on your springs.

4 Your own results.

5 The spring with the larger spring constant should feel stiffer.

6 Your own results.

19 Acceleration

Part 1: Effect of mass

1–5 Your own results.

6 a Acceleration decreases as mass increases. (Acceleration is inversely proportional to mass, but you cannot determine that the relationship is one of inverse proportion unless you plot a graph of acceleration against 1/mass and obtain a straight line.)

   b Your own answer.

7 a Your own answer.

   b The closer the data points are to the line of best fit, the better the quality of the data.

8 Your own comparison.

9 Your own answer and explanation.

Part 2: Effect of force

1–5 Your own results.

6 a The greater the resultant force on an object, the greater the acceleration of the object.

   b Your own answer.

7 a Your own answer.

   b The closer the data points are to the line of best fit, the better the quality of the data.

8 Your own comparison.

10 Your own answer and explanation.

20 Waves

Part 1

1–2 Your own results.

3 Your results may vary because of different water depths (and different values of frequency/wavelength for the series of waves).

4 There may be less than one wave in a second/any errors in counting the waves are spread out over 10 s, so this will give a more accurate value.

5 It is difficult to measure the wavelength while the waves are moving. The camera 'freezes' the motion of the waves so it is easier to make a precise and accurate measurement.

6 Your comments are likely to relate to the speed of the wave; it is difficult to measure an accurate time when something is moving fast. Suggestions could include using a video camera with a time displayed.

Part 2

1–2 Your own results.

3 You could justify either answer: the wavelength, as this is obtained from a static measurement of the rod; the frequency, as this is measured electronically.

4 Your own table.

5 The sound travels too fast to use a stop clock/human reaction time would introduce errors greater than the time being measured.

21 Radiation and absorption

1 Your own results.

2 Your graph should show curved lines with the gradient reducing as the temperature drops.

3 The rate of cooling decreases as the temperature drops.

4 You should have concluded that tubes covered with dark, dull materials are better at emitting radiation than tubes covered in light or shiny materials. Your answers should relate the emission of radiation to the cooling rates shown on your graph.

5 Your answers should discuss any anomalous (strange or unexpected) readings and how much difference in cooling rate there is between the different tubes.

6 No, only four different materials have been tested.